Louisville's First Families

SARAH VEECH GARVIN

Sketched from a portrait in the home of her granddaughter, Mary Jane Bell, on Fourth street. Sarah Veech Garvin was the daughter of John and Agnes Weir Veech and the wife of William Garvin.

Louisville's First Families

A SERIES OF GENEALOGICAL SKETCHES

BY

KATHLEEN JENNINGS

WITH DRAWINGS BY EUGENIA JOHNSON

THE STANDARD PRINTING CO.
PUBLISHERS   ::   ::   LOUISVILLE, KY.

Notice

In many older books, foxing (or discoloration) occurs and, in some instances, print lightens with wear and age. Reprinted books, such as this, often duplicate these flaws, notwithstanding efforts to reduce or eliminate them. The pages of this reprint have been digitally enhanced and, where possible, the flaws eliminated in order to provide clarity of content and a pleasant reading experience.

Copyright © 1920 by The Standard Printing Company

Originally published:
Louisville, Kentucky
1920

Reprinted:
Janaway Publishing, Inc.
2011

Janaway Publishing, Inc.
732 Kelsey Ct.
Santa Maria, California 93454
(805) 925-1038
www.janawaygenealogy.com

ISBN: 978-1-59641-243-9

Made in the United States of America

Foreword

Typical of the gentlefolk who came to the Kentucky frontier in the last thirty years of the Eighteenth century are the twelve families grouped in this series, known as Louisville's First Families. An effort has been made to picture the early social life of Louisville as inaugurated by the twelve families included and by similar families of culture and refinement that emigrated from Virginia, Maryland and Pennsylvania to the wilderness in the late seventeen hundreds.

From family records and traditions that have come down, verbally, through the several generations, material was obtained with which to illustrate the permanency of these families in the city, listing the descendants of the pioneers, to link the Eighteenth century with the Twentieth, and to indicate the shaping influence of such people upon the growth of a community.

Contents

	Foreword	7
	Introduction	13
I	The Bullitt family (part I)	19
II	The Bullitt family (part II)	27
III	The Prather family	35
IV	The Clark family	45
V	The Churchill family	59
VI	The Pope family	69
VII	The Speed family	81
VIII	The Joyes family	91
IX	The Veech family	101
X	The Thruston family	113
XI	The Taylor family	125
XII	The Bate family	141
XIII	The Floyd family (part I)	153
XIV	The Floyd family (part II)	167

Illustrations

Portrait of Sarah Veech Garvin. [Frontispiece.]

Oxmoor, the house built by Alexander Scott Bullitt.

The Jouett portrait of Cuthbert Bullitt.

The Jouett portrait of Thomas Prather.

Locust Grove, the home of Lucy Clark Croughan.

Spring Hill, the home of Samuel Churchill.

Portrait of Martha Pope Humphrey.

Farmington, the Speed homestead.

Portrait of Thomas Joyes.

Portrait of Richard Snowden Veech.

Portrait of Buckner Thruston.

Portrait of Zachary Taylor.

Portraits of Edmund Berry Taylor and his wife, Susannah Gibson Taylor.

Berry Hill, the house built by James Smalley Bate.

Portrait of John Floyd.

Portrait of Capt. Thomas Floyd Smith.

Introduction

LOUISVILLE society was as delightful in 1819 as in these 1919 care-free days of after the war, if one may rely upon the accuracy of Dr. Henrico McMurtrie, who published his "Sketches of Louisville" just a hundred years ago. Surely his graceful tribute to society will bear repetition, for while Louisville, the town of 4,500 at the Falls of the Ohio, has lost its slender proportions, has changed in many ways, even in climate, the social life has withstood time to the extent of proving quite as rare and interesting and has managed to hold within the circle families of the same name as those that dispensed hospitality in memorable fashion in his day.

Dr. McMurtrie observed that the majority of the inhabitants, engaged in adding dollar to dollar, devoted no time to literature or "to the acquirement of those graceful nothings, which, of no value in themselves, still constitute one great charm of polished society. Such is the character of the inhabitants of this place, in general, "ma ogni medaglio ha il suo reverso." There is a circle, small 'tis true, but within whose magic round abounds every pleasure that wealth, regulated by taste, can produce, or urbanity bestow.

Louisville's First Families

There, the "red heel" of Versailles may imagine himself in the emporium of fashion, and, whilst leading beauty through the mazes of the dance, forget that he is in the wilds of America."

Since that time many families have come to Louisville to take up their residence; aristocratic families of Virginia, families representing the flower of the far South, families of culture and refinement from across the Mason and Dixon line, those who came over in the Mayflower, and others on the "W. C. Hite," as one society leader cleverly described the arrival of her antecedents in our midst. These good people have made their place in the community, are indispensable to the city's business, social, and club life, but in connecting what in Dr. McMurtrie's day made society a rare and beautiful phase of life in a bustling frontier town, with the Louisville society after a hundred years have past, attention must be devoted and confined to the first families from an historian's viewpoint, but first families in the other sense, too, for they represent today what they then stood for in position, culture and refinement.

They formed the nucleus of society in 1819, but they came to the beautiful country of the Beargrass before 1800.

The population of the town in 1780 was incorrectly rated by an early historian as thirty

Introduction

inhabitants, though the figure was nearer one hundred and fifty, so it should not be difficult to separate the sheep from the goats, although it would appear that there were only sheep among the early settlers, leaving the other class to be composed of marauding Indians, who bitterly contested possession of every clearing the original group of cotillon leaders and future bank presidents made. Kentucky, at that time the Fincastle county of Virginia, was known as the land of blood, but was desired by Virginia gentlemen for immigration purposes, no less heartily than by the Indians of the North and South who had marked it for their own as a hunting ground. The Indians bit the dust in many of these encounters, but heavy toll was taken among the pioneers, whose families counted possession of Kentucky homes all the more dear in their tragic association.

"OXMOOR"

Built in 1787 by Alexander Scott Bullitt.

A view of the frame portion of the present Oxmoor house occupied by William Marshall Bullitt. The dwelling, sketched above from an illustration in Colonel Thomas W. Bullitt's "My Life at Oxmoor", included four rooms and a central hall, in which there was a stairway of walnut, prettily carved, leading to two attic rooms above.

The brick front was built by William C. Bullitt, early in the last century.

The Bullitt Family. I.

CAPT. Thomas Bullitt, a distinguished soldier in the French and Indian wars, headed a surveying party which journeyed from Virginia to the falls of the Ohio in July, 1773, and in August of that year laid out a town. Twelve years later, his nephew, Alexander Scott Bullitt, after a brief residence in Shelby county, on Bull Skin creek, moved down to the settlement at Falls of Ohio. On a farm of a thousand acres on Beargrass creek, nine miles from Louisville, he built his first home, a log cabin. He named the farm Oxmoor, from the celebrated Oxmoor, of Tristam Shandy, and on this farm lives his lineal descendant, William Marshall Bullitt, and his family, the property having been in possession of the Bullitts from that day when Alexander Scott Bullitt and his bride, Priscilla Christian, came to make the Kentucky home of this branch of the Bullitt family that has figured prominently in the social and professional life of Louisville ever since.

Alexander Scott Bullitt, the son of Judge Cuthbert Bullitt, of the General Court of Virginia, preferred coming to Kentucky to fight Indians

Louisville's First Families

to staying at home and studying law. His fifteen-year-old bride, Priscilla, was the daughter of Col. William Christian and his wife, Annie Henry, a sister of Patrick Henry. Col. Christian, by a patent of 1780, was granted 2,000 acres of the Beargrass land which had been surveyed in 1774, and on it, in 1780, there was a considerable fort, Sturgis Station, occupied by from twenty to forty families. Thither Col. Christian, of Virginia, sent his slaves ahead to prepare a dwelling, and he with his family arrived to settle in August, 1785. Col. Christian was killed by Indians in 1786. Two years after building the log cabin above the spring of Oxmoor, the Bullitts erected a frame house where their children, Cuthbert, Helen Scott, Anne and William C. Bullitt, were born.

Alexander Scott Bullitt, after the death of his wife, Priscilla, married a widow, Mrs. Mary Churchill Prather, a sister of Col. Samuel Churchill, Armistead and Henry Churchill, prominent Louisville men of affairs. The Bullitts and the Churchills were intimate friends. Alexander Scott Bullitt was one of the eleven State Senators in the first Kentucky Legislature, June 4, 1792. He was elected Speaker of the Senate and re-elected for twelve years. He was the first Lieutenant Governor of Kentucky in May, 1800. Bullitt county was named for him.

Bullitt

In September, 1819, William C. Bullitt married Mildred Ann Fry, a daughter of Col. Joshua Fry and his wife, Peachy Walker, of Albemarle county, Va., who emigrated to Kentucky, and have other descendants in Louisville in the Speeds. Col. Fry was commander of a regiment in the French and Indian war, 1754, in which George Washington served as lieutenant colonel.

William C. Bullitt built the brick front of the Oxmoor residence, completing the structure as it now stands. Here ten children were born to William C. Bullitt and his wife, and three of these have descendants in Louisville; Sue Bullitt, who married the Hon. Archibald Dixon, of Henderson, the mother of William B. Dixon; Helen Bullitt, who married Henry Chenoweth, the mother of Mrs. John Stites, Miss Fanny Chenoweth, Mrs. Hugh Barret, Mr. Henry Chenoweth and Dr. James Chenoweth; and Col. Thomas Walker Bullitt, long prominent in Louisville as a lawyer and citizen, who married Priscilla Logan. Col. Bullitt was the father of William Marshall Bullitt, Alexander Scott Bullitt and Keith Bullitt. His other children do not make their home in Louisville.

The youngest member of the family is Master Benjamin Logan Bullitt, the infant son of Mr.

and Mrs. Keith Bullitt, who leave shortly to take up their residence in Seattle.

Cuthbert Bullitt, the brother of Willian C. Bullitt, married Harriett Willett and had a son, Dr. Henry M. Bullitt, the first dean of the Kentucky School of Medicine and the city's first health officer.

Dr. Bullitt married Julia Anderson. They had one daughter, Virginia Bullitt, who married John Cood, the mother of Helen Cood, who married Owen Tyler.

Dr. Bullitt married a second time, Mrs Sallie Paradise, and had four daughters, Elizabeth Bullitt, who married Charles N. Buck, former Minister to Paris; Mrs. Julia Bullitt Rauterburg; Mrs. Edith Bullitt Jacob, wife of Mayor Charles D. Jacob, and Miss Henrietta Bullitt. Priscilla Bullitt, a daughter of Cuthbert Bullitt, married A. A. Gordon, and their daughter, Harriet, married Logan C. Murray.

The eldest child of Alexander Scott Bullitt, Anne Christian Bullitt, was married on February 4, 1819, to John Howard, of Maryland, a lineal descendant of two acting governors of that province, namely, Commander Robert Brooke and Colonel Thomas Brooke. She is ancestress of the Courtenays. Her daughter, Annie Christian Howard married October 13, 1842, Robert Graham Courtenay, of Crown Hall, Ireland, who

Bullitt

located in Louisville in 1882, subsequently becoming a prominent man of affairs, firm member of Thomas Anderson and Company, director in the Bank of Louisville, director of Louisville and Frankfort and Lexington and Frankfort Railroads, administrator of the John L. Martin estate, and president and engineer of the Louisville Gas Company. Five of their children figured in Louisville affairs.

The eldest daughter, Julia Christian Courtenay married Hector V. Loving, and has in Louisville the following children: Mrs. Julia Loving George, mother of Julia Courtenay and Robert George; Laura Loving, the wife of D. C. Harris, and Emma Loving.

Two other daughters, Emma and Helen Martin Courtenay, make their home on Fourth street.

A son, Thomas Anderson Courtenay, married Jane Short Butler, and has the following children residing here: Thomas Anderson Courtenay, Jr., William Howard Courtenay, II., and Jane Short Courtenay, wife of Henry S. Tyler.

Another son is William Howard Courtenay, chief engineer of the L. & N. Railroad, whose wife is Isabel Stevenson Clark. They have two sons, Erskine Howard Courtenay and James Clark Courtenay.

CUTHBERT BULLITT

A sketch from the Jouett portrait owned by Hugh Bullitt, the son of Mr. and Mrs. C. Malcolm Bullitt, and a great-grandson of this pioneer.

The Bullitt Family. II.

OVERSHADOWED by warehouses and office buildings, Bullitt street seems a queer memorial to those Virginia gentlemen, Cuthbert and Thomas Bullitt, who played important roles in building up a city at the falls of the Ohio, and who have left behind them, besides testimony of their useful careers, a great number of descendants who are prominent today. One wonders sometimes how it happens that this is not Bullittville. On what is now Bullitt street, back in those early days, there stood two hospitable houses, the grounds extending from Fourth to Sixth streets and with a view across the river which is now enjoyed by many business men from office windows high above the levee, then a part of the Bullitt's front lawn, for there were the homes of Mr. and Mrs. Cuthbert Bullitt, and of Mr. and Mrs. Thomas Bullitt.

The Cuthbert Bullitts had a farm about a mile and a half south of their town house, the country home being in what is now Central Park, surrounded by fields and woodland extending from Sixth to Second street. This farm, a part of the Bullitts' large holdings of real estate, was inherited by Amanthis Bullitt, who married

George Weissinger. The land was not desirable then as later when the city's growth made it necessary to drain the land, obliterating the ponds and enhancing the value of property beyond the dreams of the Weissingers, who had disposed of the farm.

In a chapter devoted to these ponds which intersected the area on which the city is built and which, breeding disease, gave Louisville the name, "Graveyard of the Ohio," Casseday wrote in his history of 1852, "A map of the city as it was sixty or even thirty years ago would present somewhat the appearance of an archipelago, a sea full of little islands. The Long Pond commenced at Sixth and Market and extended southwest to Sixteenth street. Gwathmey's, or Grayson's Pond, was on Center street just in the rear of the First Presbyterian church, which stood on Green between Sixth and Center and extended westwardly halfway to Seventh street. Besides these two principal lakes there were innumerable others, some containing water only after heavy rains and others standing full at all times. Market street from the corner of Third down was the site of one, Third between Jefferson and Green, Jefferson near the corner of Fourth and so on, ad infinitum."

Major William Bullitt was a half-brother of Capt. Thomas Bullitt, who surveyed the town in

Bullitt

1773, and of Judge Cuthbert Bullitt, the father of Alexander Scott Bullitt, another distinguished early settler. Major William Bullitt and his wife, Mary Burbridge, daughter of General Burbridge, of Warfield, Va., were the parents of Cuthbert and Thomas Bullitt, who came here in 1804, and are described in Collins' History as "two of the first merchants of Louisville distinguished for their probity and business qualifications, who amassed large estates for their descendants."

Cuthbert Bullitt married Anne Neville, of Virginia, daughter of General Joseph Neville, of Revolutionary fame. They journeyed to Louisville to build their home here on the river front. Thomas Bullitt married Diana Gwathmey, of the prominent pioneer family, and their son, Alexander Bullitt, owned the handsome home on Jefferson street, now the Holcomb mission. Alexander Bullitt married twice, his first wife being a beautiful heiress, Fannie Smith, for whom two steamboats were named, one the "Fannie Smith," the other, the "Fannie Bullitt." His second wife, also fair and rich, was Irene Williams. After this marriage he moved to New Orleans, where he bought the New Orleans Picayune, one of the biggest newspapers of the South.

Cuthbert Bullitt and his wife, Anne, were the parents of eight children, four of whom have

Louisville's First Families

families socially prominent in the city: Neville Bullitt, who married Ann Amelia Steele, the father of Neville Bullitt; William Bullitt, who married Virginia Anderson, the father of the late Alexander Bullitt, and of Malcolm and Howard Bullitt (Alexander and Malcolm Bullitt married two sisters, Clara and Heloise Kennedy); Amanthis Bullitt, who married George Wessinger, the mother of George Weissinger, who married Amelia Neville Pearce; of Blanche Weissinger, who married Capt. Thomas Floyd Smith; of Harry Weissinger, who married Isabelle Muir, and of Caroline Bullitt, who married Dr. Thomas Wilson, the mother of eight daughters.

Neville Bullitt and his wife, Ann Amelia Steele, built a country home, "Riverside," in 1830, just above the present site of the Louisville Country Club, where Mr. John H. Caperton has a handsome home now. "Riverside" was the scene of many gatherings of the Bullitts and their friends. There were eight children to grow up at "Riverside:" Neville Bullitt, Jr., who married Mattie D. Bohannon, the father of Capt. Neville Bullitt, Thomas Bullitt, of Anne Amelia Bullitt (Mrs. A. B. Pinney), and the Bullitt twins, Emily and Juliet, the latter, Mrs. James B. Ayers of Virginia; and William Wurts Bullitt, who married Medora Gilmore, the father of Medora,

Bullitt

Joseph Neville, and Kirwan Bullitt, are the only two who have families in Louisville.

Dr. and Mrs. Thomas Wilson had a daughter, Lucinda, who married Gavin Cochran. Mrs. Cochran died a short time ago, her children being: Mrs. Byron Baldwin, John Cochran, Mrs. Edmund F. Trabue and Wilson Cochran.

Almira Wilson married Lytleton Cooke, their daughter, Alice, married David Kellar; Caroline Wilson married Edward Fulton, their children being Mrs. John Tevis and Dr. Gavin Fulton; Amelia Wilson, who married Fred Anderson; Annie Wilson and Henrietta Wilson.

The children of Capt. and Mrs. Thomas Floyd Smith are: Mayor George Weissinger Smith, who married Nell Hunt, a descendant of the Prathers, another pioneer family; Mrs. Amanthis Jungbluth, Thomas Floyd Smith, who married Mary Bruce, and Nan Pope Smith, who married Frank Carpenter.

Harry Weissinger and his wife, Isabelle Muir, are the parents of Margaret, who married Samuel T. Castleman, and is the mother of Harry and Isabelle Castleman; and of Judge Muir Weissinger. Their other children do not live in Louisville.

George Weissinger, who married Amelia Neville Pearce, was the father of Amelia Weissinger, who married Hoadley Cochran. His home at

Louisville's First Families

Pewee Valley was the setting for "The Little Colonel," by Mrs. Annie Fellows Johnston, the Little Colonel being his granddaughter, Hattie Cochran, who is now Mrs. Albert M. Dick, Jr.

Benjamin Bullitt, another son of Major and Mrs. William Bullitt, married Mary Ferguson, in 1808. Their daughter, Mary Bullitt, married Major Richard Zantziger. One of their three daughters, Octavia Zantziger, married Clarence Bate, having a son, John Throckmorton Bate.

THOMAS PRATHER

This sketch is made from Jouett's likeness of this estimable gentleman, who is said to have done more for the advancement of Louisville than any other one man. The Jouett portrait of Thomas Prather is owned by his great-great-granddaughter, Mrs. J. Barbour Minnigerode.

The Prather Family.

A PUBLIC - SPIRITED citizen identified with the growth of Louisville no less than with the social life of his day was Thomas Prather, born in Maryland in 1770, of English extraction. He crossed the Wilderness Trail to seek his fortune in the new country and was one of the city's first merchants, having opened a store here as early as 1794. Success marked his every venture and riches poured in upon him. He was the capitalist of his day, and famed for his philanthropies. Broadway, for many years Prather street, was named for him. Prather was president of the first bank in Louisville, the old Bank of Kentucky, which he opened on January 1, 1812, and which did business on Main street near Fifth. When the bank suspended specie payments he resigned his office with the remark: "I can preside over no institution which declines to meet its engagements promptly and to the letter."

His generosity in contributing to charitable and civic endeavors won for him the title of "Oh, put me down for the balance," Prather. He gave five acres and Cuthbert Bullitt gave three to the city for a hospital site in 1817. Interested in the general welfare, Prather and Bullitt served on many committees together. With Peter F. Ormsby they were appointed by the Board of Trustees, in 1820, to purchase suitable fire engines (two or three), for the use of the city.

The property for the hospital site was given with the proviso that it should revert to the Prather and Bullitt heirs if used for any other purpose. When the new million dollar City Hospital was planned a change of site was considered until the deeds were looked up and disclosed this restriction. One of the numerous Prather heirs recounting the incident said "It looked for a time as if I might have fifty dollars for a new frock."

Thomas Prather was married in 1800 to Matilda Fontaine, a daughter of Capt. Aaron Fontaine, one of the pretty Miss Fontaines, as they were called, though they were also known as the alphabet Fontaines there were so many of them. Matilda and her eight sisters were all famous for their beauty and intellectuality, and all married distinguished men. From Matilda Fontaine is supposed to come the fresh blonde prettiness of the Prather women.

The Prather residence stood in Prather square, the block bounded by Third and Fourth, Walnut

Prather

and Green, Walnut street taking its name from the fine row of walnut trees on the south side of the house. This house was built by Judge Fortunatus Cosby, who married Mrs. Prather's sister, Mary Ann Fontaine.

It was on the way home from Philadelphia where he had been on business that Prather met a young man, John J. Jacob, of Hampshire county, Virginia, starting out to seek his fortune. He urged Jacob to come to Louisville, and afterward took the young gentleman into partnership, forming the firm of Prather & Jacob. John J. Jacob married Ann Overton Fontaine and built a home across Walnut street from his brother-in-law Prather's home, where the Pendennis Club is today.

Thomas and Matilda Prather had six children, two sons and four daughters. James Smiley Prather married Louisa Martin and their children were: Mary (Mrs. George Robinson Hunt) and Blanche (Mrs. Edward Mitchell). Mrs. Hunt, who died not long ago, has two daughters in Louisville—Ellen Pope Hunt, the wife of George Weissinger Smith, and Kate Hunt, who married Samuel Hutchings.

The other son, William Prather, married his first cousin, Penelope Pope, the daughter of Alexander Pope, whose wife was Martha Fontaine. This marriage establishes a wide connection of families socially prominent. William and Penelope Prather had seven daughters: Kate, who married Orville Winston; Sue, who is Mrs. John Zanone; Matilda, who married Goldsborough Robinson; Julia and Martha, who died young, and the twins, Penelope and Margaret, the latter, Mrs. John Luce, and her sister, better known as Miss Eppie Prather, the only descendant with the surname, Prather. Mrs. William B. Hardy and Humphrey Robinson are the children of Goldsborough and Matilda Robinson, who live here. Mrs. Alex P. Witty and Prather Zanone are the daughter and son of Mrs. Zanone. The daughters of Kate and Orville Winston were Penelope (Mrs. Ernest Allis), the mother of Mrs. William B. Harrison, and Kate (Mrs. Frederick Hussey), the mother of Mrs. Barbour Minnigerode, Mrs. Arthur H. Middleton, Mrs. Thomas Jefferson, of Springfield, Mass., and Mabel Hussey, of Paris.

Thomas and Matilda Prather's daughters all married prominent Kentuckians. Mary Jane Prather married Worden P. Churchill, and after his death married Dr. Charles M. Way. Her sons were Worden P. Churchill and W. H. Way.

Matilda Prather married Samuel Smith Nicholas, the distinguished lawyer and jurist. Their handsome home was on Fifth street be-

Prather

tween Chestnut and Walnut. Their daughter, Julia, Mrs. James C. Johnston, lives with her daughter, Miss Mary Johnston, at Fourth and Broadway. Their sons, George and Samuel Smith Nicholas, have a number of descendants here. George Nicholas married Emma Hawes and had a daughter, Tina Nicholas, who married John Churchill. The son of Mr. and Mrs. John Churchill is John Churchill, who married Lucy Jones.

By a second marriage to Mary Anna Pope, George Nicholas had ten children. One son, George Nicholas, who married Evelyn Thompson, lives in Crescent Hill, and another son, Pope Nicholas, lives in Shelbyville, but is in business in Louisville.

Samuel Smith Nicholas, Jr., who married Nannie Carter, daughter of Capt. Frank Carter, has two daughters in Louisville this winter, Emma Nicholas and Mrs. Harry Lee Williams, although the latter's home is in Chicago.

Maria Julia Prather married Henry Clay, Jr., the son of the Great Commoner, and her daughter, Nannie Clay, now Mrs. Henry McDowell, inherited Ashland, near Lexington, the home of Henry Clay.

Catherine Cornelia Prather married the Presbyterian minister, the Rev. Edward P. Humphrey, their son being the late E. W. C. Humphrey,

Louisville's First Families

father of Edward P. Humphrey, Lewis C. Humphrey and Dr. Heman Humphrey. Dr. Humphrey, who was a native of Connecticut and the son of a distinguished minister, the president of Amherst College, had as his charge a church in Jeffersonville at the time of his marriage to Miss Prather. Later he was minister of the old Second Presbyterian church, and this church granted him a leave of absence of eight months to go abroad after his wife's death. In 1847 he was married to Martha Pope, a daughter of Alexander Pope and Martha Fontaine, who was the widow of her cousin, Charles Pope. Dr. Humphrey and his wife, Martha Pope, had one son, Judge Alexander Pope Humphrey.

Capt. Basil Prather, born in 1740 in Maryland, was an elder half-brother of Thomas Prather. He fought through the Revolutionary war, declining any pay for his services, and later came to Louisville. He has been described as exceedingly handsome, six feet three inches tall and of cordial and engaging manners. He is numbered among the commissioners of Louisville in 1790, and owned farm land near Louisville and in other parts of the State, bequeathed to his heirs on which they settled.

At a ball given in the fort built on the site of Jeffersonville he met Fanny Meriwether, of the

Prather

pioneer family, and shortly afterward they were married. His bride was years younger than himself. They settled on a farm in the Bluegrass district, living in opulence. Their daughter, Martha Meriwether Prather, married Dr. Warwick Miller, a son of Judge Isaac Miller, of Pennsylvania, who was an early settler.

Capt. Prather died in 1803.

Richard Prather, another member of the Maryland family to settle here, was one of the "City fathers," being elected a trustee of the town of Louisville in 1797. His wife was Mary Churchill, a daughter of Armistead and Elizabeth Bakewell Churchill, of Virginia, who were among the prominent pioneers of 1787. Eliza Prather, the daughter of Richard and Mary Prather, became the wife of James Guthrie, that distinguished citizen, the founder of the L. & N. James and Eliza Guthrie had two daughters, Ann Augusta and Mary Guthrie, both of whom married and have descendants here.

Ann Augusta Guthrie married Dr. William Caldwell, and was the mother of James Guthrie Caldwell, who married Nannie Standiford; of Junius Caldwell, who married Ella Payne, of Georgetown; and of Ann Eliza Caldwell, who married Ernest Norton, and was the mother of Caldwell Norton.

Mary Guthrie married Richard Coke, of Logan county, and has a grandson, Dr. Richard Coke, who makes Louisville his home.

Mary Guthrie married a second time, John Caperton, and was the mother of John H. Caperton, who married Virginia Standiford, and has a son, Hugh John Caperton, whose wife was Dorothy Bonnie.

Following her first husband's death, Mary Churchill Prather married Alexander Scott Bullitt, this being his second marriage also.

"LOCUST GROVE"

The home of Major William Croughan and his wife, Lucy Clark.

The house, still standing, is about three fourths of a mile south of Blankenbaker's Station on the Prospect line. It was here that Gen. George Rogers Clark died on February 13, 1818.

The Clark Family.

KENTUCKY is justly famed for her hospitality, but an incident of inhospitality in a pioneer home on the Ohio river near Carrollton is the basis of an interesting anecdote for the descendants of John and Anne Rogers Clark, who emigrated from Virginia in 1784 to take up their residence at the Falls of the Ohio, where a home, "Mulberry Hill," had been made ready for them by their son, Gen. George Rogers Clark. Mr. and Mrs. Clark, their children and servants, escaped death at the hands of Indians when Mrs. Elliott, the wife of a Capt. Elliott, who had frequently been a guest at the Clark home in Caroline county, Va., failed to extend the courtesy of her house and board to them on March 3, 1785, as they voyaged down the Ohio.

The Clarks had apprised Capt. Elliott of their plans to journey to the new settlement, and had been urged by him to visit his home and to become acquainted with his wife and young daughter, of whom they had so often heard him speak. Although they left Virginia in October, owing to the bad condition of the roads, the inclemency of the weather, and the obstructions in the Monongahela, it was March when the party in boats arrived at the mouth of the Kentucky. John Clark and one of his men landing, went ahead to announce to Capt. Elliott the arrival of the party. Clark was greeted by Mrs. Elliott, who told of her husband's absence on a hunting trip. Abashed at the coolness of his reception Clark joined the travel-worn party in the boats and proceeded to Fort Nelson, where they were welcomed by the settlers.

Hardly had the Clarks resumed their journey before Indians on the war-path attacked the Elliott cabin, killing and scalping Capt. Elliott's brother, who, with several of his workmen, arrived immediately after Clark's departure to be mortified that his sister-in-law had not dispensed hospitality to the travelers. Mrs. Elliott and her daughter made a miraculous escape from the cabin to the river bank, unseen by the savages. They were joined by Capt. Elliott, who, returning unexpectedly, saw the warriors' canoes on the river and his home in flames. The Elliotts, having rescued the body of their kinsman from the ruins, embarked to seek security at Fort Nelson, where they were comforted and befriended, first of all, by the Clarks.

Mrs. Elliott offered excuses for her inhospitality, relating her confusion at the thought of receiving the Clarks in her crude frontier dwelling, know-

Clark

ing as she did the style and comfort of their life in Virginia, explaining that in years she had not seen any white persons save the members of her own family, that she was overcome with embarrassment at the encounter. She assured Mrs. Clark that the latter owed her life and that of her family to this breach of courtesy.

The pioneers John and Anne Rogers Clark had ten children, six sons, five of whom were officers in the Revolutionary war, the sixth being too young to serve; four daughters, two of whom married officers, and two soldiers in the Continental army.

Gen. George Rogers Clark, whose history-making career is too well known to be repeated here, had been in Louisville long enough to change his residence several times before his parents decided to join him, having moved with the first settler families from Corn Island in 1779 to a fort at the foot of Twelfth street, and in 1782 to Fort Nelson, built by the troops on the north side of Main street, between Sixth and Eighth.

"Mulberry Hill," a fine estate two miles east of the city limits, boasted a spacious double-log house, with a wide hall through the center. There were four large square rooms, porches and store rooms, with the kitchen in a separate building some distance from the house and near the spring.

Louisville's First Families

Gen. Jonathan Clark, who came to Louisville years later than the other members of the family, had married Sarah Hite in Virginia. He built a home at "Trough Spring," east of Mulberry Hill. The Bernheim place, Shadyside, and the old Richardson place are part of his farm. A French cabinetmaker came from New Orleans to make the furniture for his use. His daughter, Anna Clark, who married James Anderson Pearce, came into possession of "Trough Spring" and used it as a country house, her home in town being on the River front. When old Fort Nelson was razed and the property sold, Pearce bought the land and erected a brick dwelling with an iron veranda, at what is now the corner of Seventh and Water. This home, in which the Pearce children were born, was torn down when the property again changed hands, and the Burge home was built there.

James Pearce, who was a Virginian, a man of affairs and considerable means, presented the river frontage before his home, the two blocks of Water street and wharf, to the city, making a proviso in the deed which brought an interesting suit in 1880. In that year the C. & O. railroad attempted to obtain a right of way for a line along the river front and was bitterly opposed by merchants of the city who protested that the business on the wharf would be ruined by

Clark

this arrangement. A number of indignation meetings were held, attended by business men of Louisville. Temple Bodley, a young lawyer in those days, a grandson of James Pearce, was approached by a committee of merchants to ask his mother, Mrs. William S. Bodley, to file a suit to prevent this use of her father's gift, for they had found the old deed which provided that if the city permitted any building, etc., to be erected, obstructing the view of the Ohio river from the donor's home, garden or vineyard, the property should revert to the heirs. Mrs. Bodley brought the suit and an injunction was granted.

There are no descendants of Gen. George Rogers Clark in Louisville, for that distinguished member of the Clark family was never married.

Gen. Jonathan Clark and his wife, Sarah Hite, had seven children, three of whom have descendants in the city. Their eldest daughter, Eleanor Eltinge Clark, married Dr. Benjamin Temple, the prominent Methodist minister, and their family also was a large one. Their son, John B. Temple, whose third wife was Blandina Brodhead, was a prominent banker and man of affairs in Frankfort and later in Louisville, being president of the Mutual Life Insurance Company. His widow made her home in Louisville with her daughters, Mary Temple (Mrs. R. A. Robinson) and Annie Temple, her death taking place last year. Another daughter is Blandina (Mrs. William Griffiths).

Ann Clark, the third daughter of Gen. Jonathan Clark, married James Anderson Pearce, and to them eight children were born. Their son, Edmund Pearce, who married Myra Steele, was the father of Amelia Neville Pearce, who became the wife of George Weissinger, and of John C. Pearce, who married Susannah Steele. Mrs. Frank Snead, Mrs. Nolan Milton and John Clark Pearce are the children of John and Susannah Pearce, Ellen Pearce married the lawyer, Judge William S. Bodley, and was the mother of eleven children, of whom the following survive: Martha and Ann Jane Bodley, who live together on Fourth street; William Stewart Bodley, and Temple Bodley, who married Edith Fosdick.

Dr. William Clark, the son of Gen Jonathan Clark, married Frances Ann Tompkins. He inherited the Mulberry Hill home of John and Anne Rogers Clark from his father and in turn bequeathed it to his daughters, Mary, who married Dr. George E. Cooke, and Eugenia and Eliza Clark, who never married.

Dr. Clark's daughter Ellen married Newton Milton, of Memphis, and her death occurred not long ago at the home of her grandson, Karl Jungbluth, Jr., in Garvin Place. William Clark mar-

Clark

ried Annie Bailey, and was the father of Kate Clark, now Mrs. John C. Doolan, and of Louise Clark, Mrs. Harry Whitaker, of Wheeling, West Virginia.

Ann Clark, eldest daughter of John Clark, married Owen Gwathmey, and was the mother of eleven children. There are a number of her descendants in Kentucky. Samuel Gwathmey, who married Mary Booth, member of a prominent pioneer family, was the father of Rebecca Ann Gwathmey, who married Henry S. Tyler, of the distinguished family of that name and a descendant of the Oldhams. To Rebecca and Henry S. Tyler five children were born, and a number of their grandchildren are prominent here. The oldest son, Isaac Tyler, who married Jennie Owen, of St. Louis, was the father of Owen Tyler, Rebecca, Mrs. Harry L. Smyser, Isaac Tyler and the late Gwathmey Tyler, who married Edmonia Robinson. Virginia Tyler is Mrs. William A. Robinson, who with her daughter, Mrs. Spalding Coleman, makes her home on Fourth street near Kentucky. Levi Tyler married Maria Lewis and was the father of Mrs. James Franklin Fairleigh and Henry S. Tyler. Ella Tyler married Lewis H. Bond and her children who make Louisville their home are Isaac Tyler Bond, Etta, Mrs. Dudley Winston, and Joseph Bond.

Diana Moore Gwathmey, a daughter of Ann and Owen Gwathmey, was the wife of Thomas Bullitt.

Catherine Gwathmey married George Woolfolk, of the Virginia family which settled here.

Elizabeth Clark married Col. Richard Clough Anderson, who settled here in 1738. After his marriage Col. Anderson built a home in 1788, which was known as "Soldiers' Retreat," on the farm which is now owned by A. T. Hert. This country place appears on the first maps of the county.

Ann Clark, who married Owen Gwathmey, and her sister, Elizabeth Clark, who married Col. Richard Clough Anderson, are ancestresses of some Louisville families, for Anne Clark Gwathmey's daughter, Elizabeth, married her cousin, Richard Clough Anderson, Jr., who was one of the most distinguished members of the family.

Richard Clough Anderson, Jr., was an eloquent orator, an able lawyer and his talents were not confined to Louisville where he practiced law at Fifth and Main. He was Speaker of the House of Representatives and was minister to Colombia. While the Andersons were in South America two daughters were born, Elizabeth and Anne. The latter was called Anita by her nurse in Bogota, and in later life she was always Anita.

Clark

Anita Anderson was a baby when she came to the States, the mother having fallen a victim to the climate, dying at Cartagena, and it is told that little Anita came across the Isthmus of Panama, mule back, swung in a saddle bag, baby on one side and sugar on the other.

Elizabeth Anderson married Col. Stephen Johnston, U. S. N., and later L. M. Flournoy. By her first marriage there were two daughters, one, Hebe Johnston, the widow of Joseph H. Craig, of New York, is in Louisville, making her home with the Misses Blain and Judge Randolph Blain. The other daughter, Elizabeth Johnston, married Col. Julian Harrison, and one of their sons, Peyton Harrison, whose wife is Louise Wheat, has two children, Anne and Julian Harrison, and Louisville is their home.

Anita Anderson married a well-known Louisville citizen, John Thompson Gray, and a child of this marriage, Anita Gray, is the widow of Dr. James Thornley Berry, of Anita Springs, who makes her home with her daughter, Anita Berry Brooke, wife of Robert S. Brooke, of fine Virginia lineage, and a descendant of Sir Alexander Spottswood. Anne Carter, Anita Gray, Elizabeth Washington Berry, Margaret Lyle and Roberta Spottswood Brooke compose the family of Robert S. and Anita Berry Brooke.

Louisville's First Families

Not long ago, Robert S. Brooke bought some farm land in Southern Indiana, just below Fern Grove; in going over the deed to the property he found material for an interesting tradition for his family. The land is a portion of a grant to George Rogers Clark, kinsman of Mrs. Brooke, made in 1783 by Edward Randolph, Governor of Virginia, a kinsman of Mr. Brooke.

Lucy Clark, another daughter of John and Anne Rogers Clark, married Major William Croughan, who had located in Louisville as early as 1782. Their home was "Locust Grove," the scene of generous hospitality. Here Lucy Croughan's brother, Gen. George Rogers Clark, died and was buried in the old family burying ground.

Fanny Clark, the youngest of the four sisters, was married three times. The sons of her first husband, Dr. James O'Fallon, removed to St. Louis. Her second marriage was to Capt. Charles Minn Thruston, who fought in the Revolutionary war at the age of eleven years, seven months and three days. He came to Louisville about 1793. To Fanny and Charles Thruston two children were born, a son, Charles W. Thruston, and a daughter, Ann Clark.

After Capt. Thruston's death, his widow married Judge Dennis Fitzhugh. Their three children located in Arkansas.

Clark

Charles W. Thruston married Mary Churchill, the daughter of Samuel Churchill, and a descendant of the Popes and the Oldhams. Their daughter, Fanny Thruston, married Andrew Jackson Ballard, grandson of Bland Ballard, the celebrated Indian fighter. She was the mother of the late Charles T. Ballard, who married Mina Breaux; S. Thruston Ballard, who married Sunshine Harris, and Rogers Clark Ballard Thruston.

Ann Clark Thruston, the daughter of Charles Minn and Fanny Thruston, married Dr. Bernard G. Farrar, of St. Louis.

The Thruston home stood on Walnut street near Floyd, where the Ballard grandsons were born. The house was torn down in 1866, and on the site a home built by Andrew J. Ballard and his wife, was completed in 1868. The house, now used as the Detention Home, was for many years their hospitable residence.

William Clark, the youngest son, referred to above as too young to fight in the Revolution, was the explorer of the Lewis and Clark expedition from the Mississippi to the Pacific, 1804-06. He was afterward Governor of Missouri.

Gov. William Clark married Julia Hancock, of Fincastle, Va., and his son, Meriwether Lewis Clark, married Abigail Prather Churchill, of Louisville. Meriwether Lewis Clark, Jr., who mar-

Louisville's First Families

ried Mary Martin Anderson, spent a number of years in Louisville. He was one of the incorporators and the first president of the Louisville Jockey Club in 1875 when the first Kentucky Derby was run, and served as a judge at the track long after the club changed ownership.

"SPRING GROVE"

The home of Samuel Churchill and his wife, Abigail Oldham, built prior to 1804. They first lived in the little house at the left which Col. Churchill had built and occupied when a bachelor, building on a large two-story addition to accommodate their family. The house still stands, facing north on the Preston street road, just south of Eastern Parkway.

The Churchill Family.

ARMISTEAD CHURCHILL, JR., born in Middlesex, Va., in 1733, was the founder of the Louisville family of that name. He was a captain of the Farquier Militia in 1759, and served in the Revolution with the rank of colonel. Col. Churchill married Elizabeth Bakewell in 1761. They settled in Farquier county, and to them a number of children were born. In 1787, when their youngest son, Samuel, was eight years old, the Churchills started for Kentucky with their family and their slaves.

Armistead Churchill came through Cumberland Gap and across the Wilderness Trail on a coach, driving four-in-hand. On reaching Louisville he was completely disgusted with the settlement, according to a tradition in the family, and would have turned back the next day, but for three reasons: the badness of the roads over which he had traveled, the Indians that might be encountered in the forests, and the fact that the Ohio river flowed down instead of up toward Virginia. Making the best of things he stayed, settling on land nearby and southeast of the city on a plot of ground, which as "Churchill

Park" was presented to the city by his great, great grandsons, Charles T. and S. Thruston Ballard and R. C. Ballard Thruston. Armistead Churchill was buried there.

Churchill Park is now part of the Remount Station at Camp Taylor, its present employment, serving a wartime need of the government, bringing it within the definition of the city's use of the property, which was given with the proviso that it be used for either park or playground purposes.

It was this Armistead Churchill, of Kentucky, who changed the spelling of the family name which was originally Churchhill. In the Churchill Bible brought from Virginia, and which was destroyed by fire not many years ago, the names of his first five children were entered as Churchhill, while in 1770 that of Ann, the sixth child, was set down as Ann Churchill, omitting an h.

William Churchill, the grandfather of Armistead, emigrated from England in 1664 to settle in Middlesex county, Va., and to become one of the most extensive of the Virginia planters of his time. His home, Bushy Park, on the bank of the Rappahannock river near Chesapeake Bay, was noted for princely hospitality in Colonial days. A descendant, the late Charles T. Ballard, built a handsome house at Glenview, "Bushy Park," preserving the name of the Virginia home

Churchill

of his ancestor, now occupied by Mrs. Ballard and her daughter, Mrs. Charles Horner. They will move in the spring, however, for Mrs. Ballard recently sold Bushy Park to Judge Robert W. Bingham. Adjoining this estate is "Fincastle," which preserves the name of Fincastle county, Va., of which the site of Louisville was once a part, the home of another Churchill, Mrs. Alexander Pope Humphrey. On the other side of Bushy Park is Lansdowne, the home of S. Thruston Ballard, with its handsome grounds and residence.

Of the large family of Armistead and Elizabeth Churchill, three children are ancestors of Louisville folk. The fifth son, Henry Churchill, married Penelope Pope Oldham; the youngest son, Samuel Churchill, had married Abigail Oldham, the daughter of Col. William Oldham and Penelope Pope, and by his brother's marriage to his mother-in-law became her brother-in-law. To complicate the relationship of the descendants Charles T. Churchill, a son of Samuel and Abigail, married Sue Payne, granddaughter of Henry and Penelope Churchill. Henry Churchill was justice of the peace in Louisville in 1793, but in 1803 was assistant to Stephen Ormsby, judge of the first circuit court in Jefferson county. He was one of the trustees of the Jefferson Seminary in 1798, granted 6,000 acres of land by the legislature. Later Henry Churchill removed to Elizabethtown.

Samuel Churchill was a farmer and landowner who interested himself in everything designed to advance agricultural pursuits. He was also a member of the Kentucky Legislature in both Senate and House.

Henry and Penelope Pope Oldham had a son, Alexander Pope Churchill, who married Mary McKinley, the father of Mary Moss Churchill, who married her cousin, Judge Alexander Pope Humphrey; the father of Eliza Ann Churchill, who married J. B. Payne, of Elizabethtown, and was the mother of Sue Payne, who married her cousin, Charles T. Churchill. Sue Payne and Charles Churchill have a son, Samuel Churchill, who makes Louisville his home. Another descendant of Henry Churchill who came to Louisville from Elizabethtown is Mrs. Edmund S. Crume (Elizabeth Grimes), who on her mother's side is descended from the Churchills and the Paynes, and on her father's side had as a great-grandmother, Maria Mervin Fontaine, of Louisville, who married Sterling Grimes, of Georgia, and who on her wedding day rode away, never to be seen again by any member of her family.

Mary Churchill, who married Richard Prather in 1797, was a sister of Henry and Samuel Churchill and had a daughter, Eliza, who mar-

Churchill

ried James Guthrie at the home of her uncle, Samuel Churchill. James and Eliza Guthrie's daughter, Ann Augusta Guthrie, married Dr. William Caldwell, the mother of James Guthrie Caldwell, who married Nannie Standiford; of Junius Caldwell, who married Ella Payne, of Georgetown, and of Ann Eliza Caldwell, who married Ernest Norton, the father of Caldwell Norton.

Mary Guthrie married Richard Coke, of Logan county, and her grandson, Dr. Richard Coke, makes Louisville his home. Later she married John Caperton and was the mother of John H. Caperton, who married Virginia Standiford.

Mary Churchill Prather married a second time, Alexander Scott Bullitt, but there were no children of this marriage.

Samuel and Abigail Oldham Churchill had sixteen children, and their youngest, Julia, who married Dr. Luke P. Blackburn in 1857, lives in the city at her home corner of Third street and Park avenue.

Among their other children are the following, who figured in Louisville's society and civic life: Mary Churchill, who married Charles W. Thruston, mother of Fanny Thruston, who married Andrew Jackson Ballard. Fanny and Andrew Jackson Ballard were the parents of the Ballard men mentioned above.

Samuel Bullitt Churchill, who married Amelia Walker, was a prominent man of affairs in Kentucky and in St. Louis, where he edited a leading newspaper. His descendants here are the children of his son, John, and his daughter, Mary Churchill. John Churchill married Eva Ferguson and was the father of Matilda, Mrs. Herman Newcomb, and of Eva, Mrs. Frederick Smith. Mary Churchill married Dr. Richard Cowling, professor of surgery at the University of Louisville. Their children are: Matilda, Mrs. Arthur Sager; Louise, Mrs. Arthur Peter, and Amelia, Mrs. Karl Jungbluth, Jr.

William Henry Churchill was twice married; first to Kate Clark and later to Clarence Prentice's widow, Juila McWilliams Prentice. Mrs. Churchill lives with her sister, Mrs. J. H. Ranlett, on Ormsby avenue.

Abigail Prather Churchill married Meriwether Lewis Clark, but has no descendants here.

John Churchill, still another son of Samuel and Abigail, was twice married; first to a Miss Laurence, and after her death, at the age of 71, to Tina Nicholas. Their son, John Churchill, married Lucy Jones. William Henry Churchill and John Churchill had a home on Sixth street for many years, and were two of Louisville's most picturesque figures, distinguished-looking men, and practically always together. From their

Churchill

father they inherited the land which is now Churchill Downs. Charles Thruston Churchill, referred to above, married Sue Payne, and was the father of Samuel Churchill.

Emily Churchill married Hampden Zane, lived in her later life with her sister, Mrs. Blackburn, and died here a few years ago. Her descendants are in Canada.

When John Churchill married Tina Nicholas their honeymoon was spent abroad, and it so happened that they were in London at the time of Queen Victoria's Diamond Jubilee. Col. and Mrs. Churchill were given cards to the ceremony at Westminster Abbey, and upon their arrival at the entrance were asked their name by the usher, one of Her Majesty's attendants. Hearing the distinguished looking gentleman say that he was John Churchill, the usher walked backward up the aisle to the very front pews of the chapel to seat whom he believed to be a Marlborough.

William Henry and John Churchill leased their land, which is now Churchill Downs, to their nephew, Meriwether Lewis Clark, the first president of the Louisville Jockey Club. Churchill Downs in 1875 was the Louisville Jockey Club Driving Park, the name being changed afterward. The race tracks which antedate Churchill Downs were Woodlawn, on the Westport road, and

Louisville's First Families

Oakland, which was at the Seventh-street crossing. Early histories of Louisville record horse racing on what is now Market street as early as 1783, and a track at the foot of Sixteenth street, in the early part of the last century.

MARTHA POPE HUMPHREY

Daughter of Alexander Pope and Martha Fontaine, sketched from a portrait which hangs in "Fincastle", the home of her son, Judge Alexander Pope Humphrey.

Martha Pope married her cousin, Charles Pope, son of William Pope Jr., and Cynthia Sturgess. After his death, she married the Rev. Edward P. Humphrey. Judge Humphrey's wife, who was Mary Moss Churchill, is a descendant of Alexander Pope's sister, Penelope Pope, who, after the death of her husband, Col. William Oldham, married Henry Churchill. Alexander Pope Churchill, son of Henry and Penelope Pope Churchill, married Mary McKinley, and was the father of Mary Moss Churchill.

MARTHA POPE HUMPHREY

The Pope Family.

FROM Westmoreland county, Virginia, and down the Ohio to the settlement at the mouth of Beargrass, three members of the Pope family journeyed in late 1779, or in the first month of 1780, William Pope and Benjamin Pope and their sister, Jane Pope, the wife of Thomas Helm, the founder of the Kentucky family of that name. They were three of the four children of Worden Pope and Hester Netherton, John Pope, the fourth, remaining in Virginia. Worden Pope represented the fourth generation of Popes in America, before him being three Nathaniel Popes. Nathaniel Pope, I., of England, settled in Maryland prior to 1637, and was a member of the Maryland General Assembly in 1648. He moved to Virginia in 1650, and part of his estate was "The Cliffs," which passed from the Popes to one Thomas Ley, ancestor of Robert E. Lee, the name of the estate changing to "Stratford." The bricks of which "Stratford" was built are said to have been a gift from Queen Anne. Ann Pope, daughter of the first Nathaniel Pope, married John Washington, who emigrated from England and was the great-grandmother of George Washington.

Louisville's First Families

Of the three Popes who came to Louisville only one, William Pope, remained. Benjamin Pope removed to Bullitt county; Jane Pope Helm and her husband stayed only a year and then settled in Elizabethtown, establishing "Helm Place," which remained in the possession of the family until a few years ago.

It is recounted that in the year which the Helms spent in Louisville, then a most unhealthy place, they lost three small children by disease.

William Pope had married in Virginia, Penelope Edwards, a daughter of Hayden Edwards, of Farquier county, who removed to Bourbon county, Ky., to found a large and wealthy family. William and Penelope Pope had eight children, four sons and four daughters, and there are a number of descendants in Louisville. One daughter, Penelope, was the heroine of an interesting pioneer romance, and she was also one of three generations of Penelopes who were married very young, two at the age of 14, who were mothers at 15, and one married at 13, the mother of two children at 15. Coming down the Ohio river on their way to the falls of the Ohio, Col. William Pope and his family encountered a young soldier of the Revolution, Lieut. Col. William Oldham, and a warm friendship sprang up between Col. Pope and Oldham, who made part of the trip with the Pope family. Lieut.

Pope

Col. Oldham was much attracted to Penelope, the young daughter of his friend, and announced his intention of coming back to claim her for his bride, which he did three years later. Oldham was killed by Indians at St. Clair's defeat in 1791. The marriage of Penelope Pope Oldham, a widow, to Henry Churchill, and of her daughter, Abigail Oldham, to Samuel Churchill, brother of Henry, was recounted in the sketch of the Churchill family. The incident of mother and daughter marrying brothers had occurred before in the Pope family, for Hesterton Netherton Pope, after the death of Worden Pope, married Lynaugh Helm, a brother of Thomas Helm, who married her daughter, Jane Pope.

William Pope was one of the original trustees appointed by the Virginia Legislature to establish the town of Louisville in May, 1780; he made the survey of the town to carry out the plan of dividing the forfeited Connolly land into lots to be sold at $30 an acre; he was a justice of the peace in 1785. William Pope was a veteran of the Revolution, as was his brother, Benjamin, and in 1780 was made Lieutenant Colonel of the Louisville militia, to become Colonel of the same organization in April, 1784. William Pope and his family settled on the Bardstown road not far from the city limits, the house standing on what is now the country place of Mrs. Harry Bishop.

Louisville's First Families

The old Pope cemetery was on this farm, and a handsome monument stands there to mark the graves of William Pope, Jr., and his wife, Cynthia Sturgess.

In the East End there are three parallel streets, William, H and Pope streets, which make a lasting tribute to the memory of Col. Pope as an early surveyor of the town.

William Pope, Jr., and his wife, Cynthia Sturgess, had a large family, their sons and daughters marrying into families of prominence and social position, but there are few of their descendants left in Louisville. Henrietta Pope married Thomas Prather Jacob, and their home was for many years on the northeast corner of Fourth and Breckinridge. They have two sons living, Donald Jacob, who married Hallie Louise Burge, and John I. Jacob, of Louisville and Paris. Another son, the late Rev. Thomas Prather Jacob, has two children, Etta Pope Jacob and James Baird Jacob, who live with their mother, who was Martha Baird. Henry Pope, who married Alice Miller, has a daughter, Anna, Mrs. E. C. Newbold, who makes Louisville her home.

Alexander Pope married Martha Fontaine and had five children, two sons, Henry and Fontaine, who were never married, and both were killed in duels; three daughters, Penelope Pope, who married her cousin, William Prather; Martha

Pope

Pope, who married her cousin, Charles Pope, son of William and Cynthia Pope, and after his death married the Rev. Edward P. Humphrey (her only child was Judge Alexander Pope Humphrey), and Maria Pope, who married Allen P. Elston. The Elstons had a daughter, Fanny, who married Edward Payson Quigley, the mother of Eliza Quigley, Mrs. Bethel B. Veech, and of three other children who do not live in Louisville.

The numerous descendants of Penelope Pope, and William Prather were mentioned in the sketch of the Prather family.

The home of Alexander Pope, member of the Kentucky Legislature, prominent lawyer and man of affairs, stood on the south side of Jefferson street, between Sixth and Seventh, with a frontage of about 200 feet and extending back to Green street. Alexander Pope bought the property in 1806, and Judge Alexander Pope Humphrey inherited it from his mother, who was Martha Pope. Judge Humphrey was born in the old Pope home and still owns a piece of property on the block, a part of which was the lawn on the Sixth-street side of the house, retaining it for its association, and oddly enough the windows of his law office in the Inter-Southern overlook the site of the Pope house, on which is now built a row of shops.

Louisville's First Families

The Pope men were antagonists of Henry Clay and strong supporters of Andrew Jackson, and a tradition of the Popes tells of the caucus held in Alexander Pope's law office, which stood in the side yard of his home on Jefferson street, at which Andrew Jackson was brought forward as a candidate for the Presidency in 1824. When President Jackson visited Louisville he was delightfully entertained by the Pope families.

Penelope Pope, one of the four daughters of William and Penelope Pope, is the only one who has descendants here. By her first marriage to Col. William Oldham she had three children, Judge John Pope Oldham, of the Louisville Circuit Court, long prominent here; Major Richard Oldham, of the United States Army, and Abigail Oldham, who married Samuel Churchill. Judge John Pope Oldham married Malinda Talbot; their daughter, Susan Oldham, married Horace Hill, and was the mother of several children. Lily Hill married William Paca Lee and was the mother of Linda Lee, now Mrs. Thomas, and of Jouett Lee, Mrs. William Wallace, of Boston, who so frequently visits here.

Major Richard Oldham married Eliza Martin, daughter of Major Thomas Martin, U. S. A., having a son, George Oldham, who married Harriet Josephine Miller, daughter of John Adam Miller. Alfred Violett Oldham, for many years

Pope

Clerk of the City Court, is the only descendant of Major Oldham in the city.

From the marriage of Penelope Pope Oldham to Henry Churchill and from the marriage of her daughter, Abigail Oldham, to Samuel Churchill, several of Louisville's most influential families trace their lineage, the Ballards, the Humphreys, the Churchills, the Jungbluths, the Peters and others, all mentioned in the Churchill sketch.

Two sons of William and Penelope Pope, prominent men of their day, were John Pope and Nathaniel Pope, but they have no descendants in Louisville.

While Benjamin Pope and his wife, Beheathland Foote, settled in Bullitt county, near Shepherdsville, Benjamin Pope, a captain in the Revolution, was active in the shaping of the city's history. He was an ensign in Capt. James Patton's militia, and assisted in the building of Fort Nelson. He was one of Louisville trustees in 1783. Among the trustees of Louisville elected in 1809 were Benjamin Pope's son, Worden, and William Pope's son, Alexander Pope.

Worden Pope was one of three sons of Benjamin and Beheathland Pope. George and Benjamin Pope continued their residence in Bullitt county, while Worden Pope became a prominent citizen in Louisville. He was County Clerk for many years and was succeeded by his son, Edmund Pendleton Pope, and later by his son, Curran Pope, the clerkship remaining in the Pope family for over sixty years.

Elizabeth Taylor Thruston, daughter of Col. John Thruston, was the wife of Worden Pope, and there were thirteen children of this marriage. However, only three sons of the family are forefathers of Louisville people: Patrick Henry Pope, who married Sarah Lawrence Brown; Edmund Pendleton Pope, who married Nancy Johnson, daughter of Col. James Johnson; Col. Curran Pope, of the Union army, a West Point graduate, killed at the Battle of Perryville, who married Matilda Prather Jacob, daughter of John I. Jacob and Ann Overton Fontaine.

Patrick Henry Pope was the father of Edmonia Pope, who married Dr. William H. Galt, the mother of Misses Urith and Ellen Galt; and of Ellen E. Pope, who married Dr. John Thruston, the mother of Mrs. Sarah Thruston Hughes, and of Mary Anna Pope, who married George Nicholas, whose offspring is set down in the sketch of the Prather family. There were two other children who have no descendants here.

Edmund Pendleton Pope was the father of Judge Alfred Thruston Pope, legislator and jurist, who married his cousin, Mary Tyler Pope, daughter of Col. Curran Pope. Dr. Curran Pope

Pope

and Alfred Thruston Pope are the only children of Judge Alfred Thruston and Mary Tyler Pope, and live in their parents' old residence on Walnut street. Another son of Edmund Pendleton Pope is Brig. Gen. J. Worden Pope, U. S. A., retired, whose home is in Denver. Gen. Pope was at one time quartermaster general of the army, and was for a time commandant of the disciplinary barracks at Ft. Leavenworth. His son, Worden Pope, spent the autumn in Louisville at Camp Taylor in the F. A. R. D., and was a candidate officer in the artillery school when the armistice was signed.

Mary Tyler Pope, the mother of Dr. Curran Pope and Alfred Thruston Pope, was the only child of Col. Curran Pope, with descendants here.

"FARMINGTON", THE SPEED HOME

A sketch made from a photograph used to illustrate Hay and Nickolay's "Life of Lincoln". Some years before the war, Lincoln made an extended visit to the Speeds at the old home, "Farmington", which was built about 1810.

The Speed Family.

THE recurrence of the given names of James and John in the Speed family, generation generation, is a striking point in the study of the Speed genealogy. It was a John Speed, son of James Speed, who founded the Louisville family just at the beginning of the Nineteenth century, and who built in 1810 the historic home of the Speeds—"Farmington"—five miles from the courthouse, out on the Bardstown road.

Capt. James Speed, son of John Speed and Mary Taylor, was born in Mecklenburg county, Va., married Mary Spencer, of Charlotte county, served in the Revolution, and in 1782 came to Kentucky. In that year his son, John Speed, afterward Judge Speed, of Louisville, was ten years old. Capt. Speed, with his wife and six children, crossed the Wilderness road and settled near Danville. One son, Thomas Speed, moved to Bardstown, but was in business at Shepherdsville with his brother, John Speed, who, inheriting farm land from his father's handsome estate in 1800, established himself in Jefferson county. John Speed served in the United States forces in 1791 against the Indians.

"Farmington" in Judge John Speed's life was the scene of lavish hospitality extended not only to kinsmen and friends, but even to an army, for, it is said, that the volunteers for the War of 1812, passing "Farmington," were entertained in entire companies and even larger bodies of men.

Judge Speed was twice married, his first wife being Abby LeMaster, whose two daughters were never married; his second wife was Lucy Gilmer Fry, one of the daughters of Joshua Fry and Peachy Walker, a descendant of Dr. Thomas Walker, the earliest explorer in Kentucky, and a sister of Mary Ann Fry, who married William Christian Bullitt.

Lucy Gilmer Fry came to Kentucky with her parents, who settled in Mercer county, and it was an odd coincidence of her marriage that like her husband she was just ten years old when her family immigrated to the new country. Her middle name, Gilmer, has proven a favorite with the Speeds, and it occurs in several branches of the family today. To John and Lucy Speed eleven children were born, and at a gathering of their offspring in 1881, at a Fourth of July picnic, 107 members of the Speed family in Louisville attended.

It was to "Farmington" that Abraham Lincoln came before the Civil War to visit his friend, Joshua F. Speed, the fifth son of Judge Speed. The friendship, which was one of Lincoln's

Speed

strongest attachments, was the result of a meeting in Springfield, Ill., where Joshua Speed spent seven years in his early manhood. He became one of Louisville's foremost business men, and his wife, Fanny Henning, of fine Virginia stock, shared her husband's popularity. She was the sister of James W. Henning, with whom her husband was in partnership in the real estate business. She had no children.

The old home of Joshua F. Speed was "Cold Spring," on the road from the city to "Farmington." Remodeled and with numerous additions the old house is incorporated in the present home of Mrs. Samuel C. Henning, near Cherokee Park. Mrs. Henning is not a Speed, but her brother, Calvin Morgan Duke, who lives in Ohio, married Jennie Speed, daughter of George Keats Speed and Jennie Ewing, and granddaughter of Major Philip Speed. The late Samuel C. Henning was a nephew of Fanny Henning Speed.

Seven children of Judge John Speed's family of eleven children have descendants here: James Peachy, William Pope, Susan Fry, Philip J. Smith and Martha B. Speed. James Speed, born in 1812, was Attorney General in Lincoln's cabinet, was a widely known lawyer, partner of Chancellor Henry Pirtle, and was mustering officer for the United States army in the Civil War. All the Speeds were loyal Unionists. James

Speed married Jane Cochran, daughter of John Cochran, and had a hospitable home at Sixth and Walnut. They had a country home on the site of "Campo Bello," the home of John M. Atherton, near Cherokee Park.

James Speed served in the Kentucky Legislature and was a member of the faculty of the law department of the University of Louisville. James and Jane Speed had six sons, three of whom live in Louisville: John Speed, who married Aurore Combs, father of James Speed, who married Jane Barker; and Charles Speed, who married Eliza Homire, and has two daughters here, Bessie and Helen Speed; and of James Speed, who married Hattie Morton, father of Hallie, Mrs. Karl Harris, and of Nellie, Mrs. Edward Ream. In this branch of the family, as in many of the others, there are children and grandchildren living, but not in the city of Louisville, to which these sketches are confined.

James Speed, whose wife is Jane Barker, and who is frequently called the "bird man," compiled the material for the book, "James Speed, a Personality," privately printed by Hattie Bishop Speed after the death of her husband, James Breckinridge Speed, who had collected a great deal of material, and a number of papers and letters with the idea of publishing a life of his uncle, James Speed.

Speed

Peachy Speed named for her ancestress, Peachy Walker, married Austin Peay, and her daughter, Eliza Peay, married Col. John H. Ward. Ossian Ward, who married Mabel Prettyman, and John Hardin Ward, who married Letty Lee Peter, are her only grandchildren in Louisville. Visiting here at present is another granddaughter, Frances Hartwell, of Cambridge, Mass., daughter of Alice Peay and Dr. Samuel Hartwell.

William Pope Speed, named for Col. William Pope, the pioneer, married three times, and by his second wife, Mary Ellen Shallcross, had one son, James Breckinridge Speed, the successful banker and capitalist, who married Cora Coffin, of Cincinnati, having two children, Olive Speed, who married Frederic M. Sackett, and William Shallcross Speed, who married Virginia Perrin. J. B. Speed married a second time, his widow being Hattie Bishop Speed.

Susan Fry Speed married Benjamin O. Davis, of Boston, who located in Louisville and was partner of William H. Pope in the Pope-Davis Company. Their daughter, Lucy Gilmer Davis, married J. Edward Hardy, and is the mother of Charlotte Hardy, Mrs. Charles Pettet Robinson, of Lucy Hardy, Mrs. T. C. Hobbs, of William B. Hardy, who married Julia Robinson; of the Rev. Frank Hardy and of Kate W. Hardy, who married Gen. J. M. Califf. Kate Davis married

Dexter Hewett and was the mother of Leonard Hewett, who married Margaret Fink, and of Henry Hewett, who married Bertha Cooper.

Jane Lewis Davis married Dr. Douglas Morton and is the mother of Edward Davis Morton, who married Austine Barton (their children are Henrietta Barton Morton and Susanne Speed Morton, the latter, aged five weeks, being the youngest member of the Speed family); of Dr. David Cummins Morton, who married Mary Ballard, their children, Thruston, Jane and Rogers Morton, are descended from the Clarks, Churchills and Popes, as well as the Speeds) and of Lewis D. Morton, who married Mary Marple.

Major Philip Speed, born in 1819, served in the Federal army as paymaster. His wife was Emma Keats, a niece of John Keats, the poet. Their home was on Walnut street, near Eighth street, and they entertained extensively. They lived afterwards on First street, rearing a large family. Their daughter, Mary Speed, married Enos Tuley, the mother of Philip Speed Tuley, who married Lida Swope; of Dr. Henry Enos Tuley, who married Ethel Brown Engelbach; of Thomas Speed Tuley, who married Betty Watkins.

Ella Keats Speed married Thomas Crutcher, and was the mother of Emma Keats Crutcher, who married James Gardner; of Thomas B.

Speed

Crutcher, who married Pearl Robb; of Mary Crutcher, who married Will Parker; of Philip Speed Crutcher, who married Anna Hall.

Alice Speed married Harry P. McDonald, and has a daughter, Fanny S. McDonald.

Thomas A. Speed married Amelia Harrison (now Mrs. Edgar J. Levey), and was the father of Meta duPont Speed, Mrs. Guy Warren, and Mary Tuley Speed, Mrs. Sam Young Bingham.

J. Smith Speed married Elizabeth Williamson, and there were no children of this marriage; later he married Susan Philips, and their oldest child, named Elizabeth Williamson Speed, married Richard Jouett Menefee, and was the mother of Margaret, Mrs. James Ross Todd, of Richard H. Menefee, who married Edith Norton, and of three other sons who do not make Louisville their home.

Joshua Speed, who married Carrie Nicholson, is the only one of J. Smith Speed's four sons located here. His children are: Evarts Speed, who married Mildred Vaughan; Susan Philip Speed and Abby Nones Speed.

Martha B. Speed, the tenth child of John an Lucy Speed, married Thomas Adams, and wa the mother of Gilmer Speed Adams, who ma ried Lettie Robinson.

Major Thomas Speed, Revolutionary soldie the elder brother of Judge John Speed, who home was "Cottage Grove," at Bardstown, has several descendants in the city. By his second marriage to a widow, Mary McElroy Allen, he had a son, Thomas Spencer Speed. Thomas Spencer Speed married, first, Sarah Whitney Sparhaw, and their son was Thomas Speed, one of Louisville's finest citizens. He was a leading lawyer and for years clerk of the Federal Court. His wife was Lucy Buckner Speed, and for years their home was on Fourth street opposite Central Park. Mary Whitney Speed, a daughter, lives here. In her possession is the Speed Bible, in which eight generations have been entered. Thomas Speed's "Records and Memorials of the Speed Family" is a prized possession in the American homes of the Speeds.

By a second marriage to Margaret Hawkins, Thomas Spencer Speed had three children, Austin P. Speed, whose widow, Georgia McCampbell Speed, lives in the city; Canby Speed, who married Emma Fullinwider, the father of Mary Louise, Margaret and Emily Speed, and Capt. William Speed, whose wife was Helen Harthill; and of Louise Speed, who makes her home with her three nieces.

The Speeds trace their lineage from John Speed, the historian and geographer of the Elizabethan age.

THOMAS JOYES

Sketched from a portrait owned by this distinguished citizen's grandson, Chapman C. Joyes.

Thomas Joyes was the eldest son of Patrick Joyes, founder of the Louisville family, was a noted linguist, fought in early wars, and was identified with the social and political life of old Louisville.

The Joyes Family.

IT was after only three years in America that Patrick Joyes, of Galway, Ireland, cast his lot with the pioneers, reaching Louisville in the year 1784. This Irish gentleman, after completing his education in France and Spain, lived for some time in France, and with his wife, Anne O'Gara, of Ireland, sailed from Bordeaux and took up his residence in Philadelphia. Making a business trip to the Falls of the Ohio, he decided to settle here, and his first home, on the northeast corner of Sixth and Main, remained in the possession of the family for 99 years.

The home of Anne and Patrick Joyes was famed for the hospitality of colonial days, so little understood by the most genial host of the present, with parties of friends and later of kinsmen, arriving on horseback and by stage coach from Virginia and the Central Kentucky settlements, assured of hearty welcome. Those were the days of the trundle beds and of huge bedrooms accommodating two or more of the old four posters, one of which slightly crowds the sleeping apartments of today. The style of entertaining continued in the Joyes family to the time when horseback rides were replaced by journeys on steam cars. In 1892, at the country home of Patrick Joyes II, near Shelbyville, called "Oxford" for his grandfather's boyhood home in Ireland, lavish hospitality was the echo of the century before. It was at "Oxford" that the second Patrick Joyes, with his family, spent the last twelve years of his life.

The Joyes family is entirely distinct from the family of Joyce, whose name is pronounced the same way, and, in fact, with the exception of an army officer, who emigrated from Galway much later than the Louisville settler, there are no other Joyeses in the States beside the descendants of Patrick and Anne Joyes, and comparatively few of them.

Two sons and three daughters were born to the pioneer couple at the home at Sixth and Main. All married and lived in either Louisville or Jefferson county. Thomas Joyes, born in 1789, the elder son, is said to have been the oldest male white child born within the city limits. Like other patriotic citizens of his time, he had ample opportunity for military service, figuring in the Wabash Campaign of 1812, and with the rank of captain fought with the 13th Kentucky militia at the Battle of New Orleans.

He was a surveyor and spent part of his young manhood in the office of the county clerk. He was sent to the Kentucky Legislature several times.

Joyes

He was one of the Louisville citizens to be pallbearer at the re-interment of Daniel Boone's body at the Frankfort cemetery in 1845.

Thomas Joyes was noted as a linguist, inheriting the gift from his father, who spoke French, Spanish and German fluently. To these his son added several Indian dialects, and it was of him that Judge Fortunatus Cosby said he believed if Tom Joyes was shut up over night in the room with a Russian he would be in full command of the language by break of day. His early holdings were Jacob's Park, then Burnt Knob, a farm of over 300 acres, and the major portion of Towhead Island (the Guthrie heirs and the widow of the Rev. John Norton owned a small part of the island). Burnt Knob was sold by Patrick Joyes II to the city for park purposes when Mayor Charles Jacob was in office.

Thomas Joyes married Judith Morton Venable, daughter of Judge Joseph Venable, of Shelbyville, and had one child, Patrick Joyes, born in 1826, at his grandfather's home on Main street. He was educated at Centre College and was a graduate of Harvard Law, was a public-spirited citizen and one of the first presidents of the Y. M. C. A. He was also the first president of the Charity Organization, now the Associated Charities, served on the board of the Cook

Benevolent Fund Home for the Aged, and was an elder in the First Presbyterian church.

Patrick Joyes married Florence Coleman, a great beauty and a greatly beloved woman, daughter of Chapman Coleman and his wife, Anna Mary Crittenden. Their hospitable home was on Second street, next door to Christ Church Cathedral House. They were the parents of six children. Their daughter, Anna Mary Joyes, married Haiden Trigg Curd, the mother of Florence Joyes Curd; Mrs. Percy N. Booth, who has two children, Florence Joyes and Alexander Galt Booth; of Pattie Curd, Mrs. Albert Hueling Davis, of Jacksonville, the mother of Albert Hueling Davis, Jr.; of Lieut. Joyes Curd, United States Air Service, recently returned from France and now at a rest camp in the Catskills. Lieut. Curd was gassed while on duty over there.

Chapman C. Joyes married Sallie Swope, daughter of Ben L. Swope, and is the father of Janet Staines Swope and of Thomas Swope, who has just been released after two years' military service.

Capt. Morton Venable Joyes, Judge Advocate's Department, Washington, married Caroline Hancock Barr, daughter of Judge John W. Barr, and is the father of Lieut. Watson Joyes, U. S. Engineers, in France, of Preston Pope Joyes, who married Nina Harlan Bingham, the father of Nina and Preston Pope Joyes, of Florence Coleman Joyes, II, and of Morton V. Joyes, Jr.

Florence Coleman Joyes I, and Patrick Joyes, Jr., make their home with their sister, Mrs. Curd, on First street, and another brother, Dr. Crittenden Joyes, who married first Lida Robinson, daughter of Worthington Robinson, and later married Almeda Griggs, of Texas, lives in Fort Worth and is the father of one child, Mary Griggs Joyes.

Catherine Joyes, daughter of Patrick and Anne O'Gara, married William McGonigale, and was the mother of John McGonigale, of the old surveying and real estate firm of Henning, McGonigale & Hobbs. He married Josephine Miller Oldham, widow of George Oldham, and his children are William J. McGonigale, Florence Joyes McGonigale and Mary McGonigale.

Nancy Joyes married Thomas Johnson, of Jefferson county, and was the mother of Thomas Johnson, who married a sister of E. D. Standiford.

Thomas Johnson III married Betty Brooks, the father of Brooks Johnson, of Edward Lee Johnson and of Etta Brooks Johnson, Mrs. Edward C. Tyler.

Elizabeth Joyes married William H. Sale and was the mother of William H. Sale, who mar-

Louisville's First Families

ried Della Nagle, father of Della Sale, Appeline Joyes Sale and of Hewett Sale, of Chattanooga and Louisville. Another grandchild is Betty Sale Reese, widow of Edward Reese, whose father was Charles Sale.

John Joyes, the youngest child of Patrick and Anne Joyes, was born in 1799, was educated at St. Mary's College, studied and practiced law, was the second Mayor of Louisville, and City Judge from 1835 to 1854. He married Harriet Lanier, daughter of Major Thomas Martin Lanier, distinguished soldier of the Revolution. His daughter, Stella Joyes, married James A. McAfee, of pioneer family, and was the mother of Annie McAfee, who married Robert Dulaney, and has one son, Woodford Dulaney, recently returned from service overseas, and of Leal McAfee.

Judge Joyes' daughter, Susan Joyes, married Major Edward P. Byrne, of the Confederate Army, and her daughter, Harriet, married Heaton Owsley, and was the mother of Edna Owsley, Mrs. Frederic Hill, of Chicago, and of John Owsley, of New Haven, Conn., whose wife was Helen Hall.

A son, Clarence Joyes, married Mary Riddle and has a son, William Joyes, who makes St. Louis his home. Judge Joyes' other sons were gallant soldiers in the Confederate army: Capt.

Joyes

Erskine Joyes, who was killed in action, attached to Second Kentucky Regiment; Lieut. John Joyes, who served under his brother-in-law, Major Byrne, who commanded a Kentucky Battalion.

RICHARD SNOWDEN VEECH

Sketched from a picture made on the day of his wedding to Mary Louise Nichols. Five of his six children make Louisville their home.

The Veech Family.

JOHN VEECH, born in Ulster, Ireland, in 1747, emigrated in his early manhood to settle in Pennsylvania. He was a surveyor by profession, and colonial records show that he was making surveys in what is now Jefferson county as early as December 21, 1785, on a permit from William and Mary College, signed by Thomas Jefferson.

On his arrival in the colonies, John Veech joined a Scotch Presbyterian settlement at Uniontown, Pa., and it was there that he married Agnes (Nancy) Weir. They came to Kentucky shortly after the Revolution, down the Ohio river, it is understood, on flat boats to Falls of the Ohio. Their first child, Alexander Veech, was born January 27, 1787, in Dutch Station, one of the historic forts which were refuge for the pioneers. The first Veech farm was on the Shelbyville road about a mile above St. Matthews, and some two miles from the old station and from "Indian Hill," which was the home of Alexander Veech, and has never passed out of the family, now being occupied by James Nichols Veech and his family.

John Veech bought "Indian Hill" (of 324 acres, the old deed states) on December 1,

Louisville's First Families

1806, from Richard Taylor. The Veech family kept the property until 1814, when they sold to Zachary Taylor, son of Richard Taylor, founder of the Kentucky family. There is a tradition that when John Veech offered the Indian Hill farm to Alexander Veech, the son refused it because he said it was too far from his parents' home. It seems that a dense forest stood between the two farms. However, in 1833, Alexander Veech purchased the Indian Hill farm which was to be his life-long home.

John and Agnes Veech had five children, three of whom left descendants, but only two had families which figure in Louisville life—Alexander Veech and his sister, Sarah Veech, who married William Garvin. Agnes Veech died in 1811, John Veech in 1817.

Alexander Veech was a youthful Kentucky volunteer in the War-of 1812, fighting in the Battle of the Thames. From early manhood he was called Capt. Veech, having commanded a home-guard which offered defense against Indian raids. It is interesting to know that the Veech farm was named Indian Hill because of the marauders' headquarters located there when planning an attack upon Louisville. Two fine springs on the place proved a drawing card to the Indians when selecting a point for an encampment.

Veech

One of these springs near the Veech home has furnished drinking water for the family through several generations. The Indians chose the hill as a gathering point, and they deadened the lumber on this prominence as a forest signal to the braves. "Indian Hill" is on the Brownsboro road, and the rolling farm-land adjoins the golf links of the Louisville Country Club, which lies between the farm and the river.

Alexander Veech married Olivia Winchester, daughter of Richard Winchester, pioneer from Maryland, in May, 1821, at the Winchester home, Vale of Eden, near Lyndon, afterwards buying out the other heirs and making it their home until about 1832, when they took possession of "Indian Hill." The large white brick house on "Indian Hill" in which Richard Snowden Veech was born in 1833 was added on to by this member of the family in 1881, when a wing was built at the side and the main entrance changed. This house is still occupied by Veeches.

To Alexander and Olivia Veech were born four children, but Richard Snowden Veech was the eldest child, the only one to leave descendants. Born at "Indian Hill," when he died in 1918 he had known no other home. Like the father and grandfather before him, he loved the land and farmed the acreage around his home, after being educated at Centre College. When the farmers of four counties, Jefferson, Oldham, Bullitt and Shelby, organized the Farmers and Drovers' Bank, Richard Veech was made cashier and was active in its management from 1868 until 1880, when he became president of the New Albany and Monon Railroad. While he was in business in Louisville for some twenty years, he was best known as the distinguished horse breeder, and he built up a reputation for Indian Hill Farm from coast to coast, as the home of fine trotting stock.

He established the Indian Hill Farm in 1872, putting at the head of the breeding farm, Princeps, a descendant of Woodford Mambrino, who was the most prominent branch of the Mambrino Chief family, which was at that time one of the most prominent factors in the trotting horse world.

While 1878 was the banner year of the famous stock farm, breeding trotters was a lucrative business there for twenty years and with the horse interest a picturesque life set in at Indian Hill. Because the land was very rolling, a half mile straightway dash was used for training; there were generally from fifty to sixty brood-mares on the farm.

From 1878 to 1885, particularly, and in other years, also, prominent business men and horse

Veech

breeders of the East, from New York, Boston and Philadelphia, made a practice of forming private-car parties (usually of two cars) to visit Louisville before going to the Lexington trot meeting. Here they would be entertained at dinner by Richard Veech and by John B. Mc-Ferran, who at that time. owned fine trotting stock at Glenview Farms. The horse-lovers would visit the two farms and would attend the sales which Messrs. Veech and McFerran would hold in conjunction at Indian Hill or Glenview. These sales were attended by horse-breeders from all over the country.

Veech and McFerran belonged to Kentucky's big six, which included, besides themselves, Henry Clay McDowell, of Ashland; A. J. Alexander, of Woodford; E. G. Stoner, of Bourbon, and Lucas Brodhead, of Versailles.

In 1881 Richard Veech acquired the Beargrass farm of 700 acres, of which he used a portion for cultivation, with part in pasture and the remainder set aside for training purposes. This farm includes the ground upon which Dutch Station stood, and is now owned by Bethel B. Veech, who was associated with his father in conducting the stock farm from 1882 to 1897. Bethel Veech has a summer bungalow not far from the site of the old fort. Another pioneer fort, Cane Station, stood about midway the Indian Hill farm, and it is told that in recent years while plowing a portion of the land a number of Indian arrowheads were turned up.

An interesting and unusual incident of Richard Veech's career as a horseman occured in 1918, the last year of his life. While ill at a hospital in the city he prepared from memory a pedigree list of some fifty head of trotting stock, still at Indian Hill, furnishing a record of each animal described to him, and, before his death, arranging a sale of these horses.

Richard Snowden Veech married Mary Louise Nichols, of Danville, Ky., whose parents were of Puritan stock from Rhode Island. The six children of this marriage are living, five of them in Louisville, the home of one daughter, Mrs. A. Hunter Kent, being St. Louis.

Elizabeth Veech is the wife of Burwell K. Marshall, and the mother of Richard Veech Marshall, of St. Louis, whose wife was Helen Chauncey, of Olney, Ill.; of Elizabeth and Louise Marshall, now in France on Red Cross service; of Sallie Ewing Marshall, the wife of Nicholas Dosker, and of Burwell K. Marshall, Jr.

Olivia Winchester Veech, Mrs. Kent, has one daughter, Mary Kent, the wife of Major Manton Davis and the mother of Olivia Davis.

Bethel B. Veech married Eliza Quigley and has one daughter, Elston Veech, wife of William

Veech

Mills Otter, who has two small children, Bethel and Ann Otter.

Helen Lee Veech is the wife of George Twyman Wood and has three sons, George Twyman Wood, Jr., who married Louise Robertson, of Washington, and makes New York his home, Richard Veech Wood and Thomas J. Wood, who is a student at Princeton.

James Nichols Veech married Agnes Ross, makes Indian Hill his home, and farms as his father and grandfather before him. He is the father of Agnes Veech and of John Alexander Veech, named for John Veech and Alexander Veech.

Dr. Annie S. Veech, who makes Louisville her home, has been on duty overseas with the Red Cross.

Sarah Veech, daughter of John and Agnes Weir Veech, born in 1795, was the bride of William Garvin, an Irishman from County Derry, born the same year as she, and emigrating to this country to settle in Philadelphia for a brief time before coming to Shelbyville, Ky. Sarah Veech and William Garvin were married January 2, 1822, at the home of the bride's older sister, Mrs. Francis Veech Brookey in Shelbyville, and on horseback the young couple left for Glasgow, their wedding journey to the new home being made in the saddle, despite the bitter weather of mid-winter.

Four children were born to the Garvins at their Glasgow home, which they left in 1827 to locate in Louisville. They bought a home on Jefferson street, between Fourth and Fifth, and they became identified with the social life of the city. William Garvin engaged in the wholesale dry goods business, and was a successful merchant of Garvin, Chambers & Co. and later of Garvin, Bell & Co.

In 1852, the Garvins moved further out in town to a home on Chestnut street, which was to be the scene of elaborate entertaining for four generations of the family.

For this home William Garvin found many beautiful things, objects of art from abroad. Two marble mantels from Italy, exquisitely carved and intended for the Chestnut street house were among the handsome fittings brought from Philadelphia, through the Erie Canal and over the mountains in wagons. These mantels are now in the home of William Garvin's granddaughter, Mrs. Crittenden Taylor Collings, on Spring Drive.

Sarah Veech and William Garvin had three children, Jane Orr Garvin, Ann Eliza Garvin and Emmet Garvin. The daughters married brothers, John and Robert Bell, from Ireland.

Veech

Jane Orr Garvin and John Bell purchased the Hunt house (now the Pendennis Club) and this was their home in the sixties. During the Civil War, John Bell receiving word that his brother, Lieut. William Bell, of the Confederate army, had been wounded, left for the South in search of him. John Bell was not destined to find his brother, and stricken ill on a train in Alabama, died and was buried in that State, many weeks before his family received news of his death. Lieut. Bell, fatally wounded at the Battle of Shiloh, was taken to the home of his cousin, Samuel Gwyn, at Memphis, where he died.

William Garvin lost his life in the steamboat disaster on the Ohio in 1868, when the United States and the America collided. His body was washed ashore, and clasped in his hands was found the Bible which he had been reading. He was an elder in the Presbyterian church with which his family and the Veech family have been identified in this city.

Ann Eliza Garvin, who married Robert Bell, inherited the Chestnut street house and lived there until her death in 1911. Jane Garvin Bell with her children returned to this house after the death of her husband, but later lived on Third street, and at an advanced age she died there in 1918.

Louisville's First Families

Jane and John Bell were the parents of Garvin Bell, who married Ellen Robinson, and was the father of Nelchen Bell, Mrs. Alex Galt Barret, of Louise Bell, Mrs. Howard Lee; of Madeline Bell, Mrs. Robert F. Vaughan; of Robert Bell, of Florida, and Francis Bell.

Jane and John Bell's daughter, Mary Jennie Bell, makes Louisville her home, and with her, a niece, Jeannette Garvin Payne, daughter of Elizabeth Bell and Henry Payne, of Georgetown, the sons of this marriage being Thomas Henry Payne, of Winnipeg, who married Amelia Brown, a descendant of a sister of William Garvin and John Payne, whose home is New York.

John Stuart Bell and Sarah Francis Bell, both dead, were children of Jane and John Bell.

Ann Eliza Garvin and Robert Bell had three children, Annie Garvin Bell, the wife of Crittenden Taylor Collings, and mother of Edith Collings Fisk, in France on Red Cross duty, of Allison Collings, and of Christine Collings, wife of William Hall, and with her husband and children, Edith and Noel, makes her home at Short Hills; Catherine Gwyn Bell, widow of Foster Thomas, who with her son, Garvin Thomas, lives in France, and Henry Bell, deceased.

Emmet Garvin married Lucy Tomlinson, and their daughter, Sarah Garvin, is the widow of General John F. Weston, and is in New York with her daughters, Marie and Kathleen Weston.

JUDGE BUCKNER THRUSTON

Senator from Kentucky, 1804-1809, retired to become United States Judge for the District of Columbia, 1809-1845, appointed by President Madison. He was succeeded in the Senate by Henry Clay.

Judge Thruston was one of three sons of the Rev. and Col. Charles Minn Thruston, who came to Kentucky, inheriting their father's lands in this state.

The Thruston Family.

THE English Thrustons laid great stress on family records, and as early as the Seventeenth century kept a genealogy which has been handed down from father to son, and after remaining in Louisville for three generations is now in the possession of Dr. Charles Minn Thruston, of Waco, Tex. Thanks to this old record book the genealogy of the family is unusually complete, and the Kentucky family has not neglected to keep up the tradition chronicling the history of fighters and lawyers, men of affairs and of beautiful women.

Col. John Thruston, of the third generation at Gloucester Point, Va., married Sarah Minn and had only one son, Charles Minn Thruston, who was known as the fighting parson of the Revolution, although he was officially the Rev. and Col. Thruston. He was educated at William and Mary College, and studying for the ministry, went to England to take orders. He moved from Gloucester Point to the Shenandoah Valley, and the old church at Berryville, where he preached, is still standing. His military career started at the age of twenty, when as a lieutenant of Provincials he took part in the campaign which resulted in the evacuation of Fort Duquesne. When the Revolution broke out he exhorted the Virginia youths to enlist, and at the head of a regiment joined Washington in New Jersey.

The Rev. and Col. Thruston married, first, Mary Buckner, by whom he had three sons— John, Buckner and Charles Minn Thruston, to whom he left his lands in Kentucky. He married a second time Ann Alexander, and removed to Tennessee and later to Louisiana, where he lived on a plantation until his death, in 1812.

John Thruston and Charles Minn Thruston came to Louisville, while Buckner Thruston settled in Lexington. John Thruston came west as a lad of 16 to fight under Gen. George Rogers Clark in the Illinois regiment. He served in the campaigns against Kaskaskia and St. Vincents (Vincennes), with the rank of cornet. He received in 1831 a grant of 2,666 acres of land in Illinois under the Virginia act of 1779, which provided that the volunteers (officers and soldiers), who served through the campaign which reduced the British forts in Illinois, should receive remuneration in land.

John Thruston, who came to Louisville in 1789, married his cousin, Elizabeth Thruston Whiting, and their home was "Sans Souci," which stood on the site of "Hayfield," the home

Thruston

of Mrs. Robert Tyler. They had ten children, but of these only two are ancestors of Louisville folk, Elizabeth Taylor Thruston, who married Worden Pope, of the pioneer family, and Charles Minn Thruston, who married Eliza Sydnor Cosby, daughter of Judge Fortunatus Cosby, and his wife, Mary Ann Fontaine.

After the death of John Thruston, his widow married Capt. Aaron Fontaine, the grandfather of her son's wife.

Elizabeth Taylor Thruston and Worden Pope had three sons. Patrick Henry Pope married Sarah Lawrence Brown, and was the father of Edmonia Pope, who married Dr. William Galt, their children being Ellen Galt and Urith Galt; of Ellen E. Pope, who married Dr. John Thruston; of Mary Anna Pope, who married George Nicholas, and was the mother of George Nicholas and Pope Nicholas.

Edmund Pendleton Pope married Nancy Johnson, and was the father of Judge Alfred Thruston Pope, who married his cousin, Mary Tyler Pope, their children being Dr. Curran Pope and Alfred Thruston Pope. Mary Tyler Pope was the daughter of Col. Curran Pope and Matilda Prather Jacob.

Charles Minn Thruston, born in 1793 at Sans Souci, was a celebrated criminal lawyer in Louisville. He and wife, Eliza Sydnor Cosby, had

Louisville's First Families

a large family, and there are in Louisville descendants of three of their children. Their daughter, Mary Thruston, married Dr. Lewis Rogers, the well-known physician, and was the mother of six children. Jane Farrar Rogers married Robert Atwood, her children being Lewis R. Atwood, Lizzie Atwood, Mrs. Oscar Beckmann, William Atwood, who married Nellie Stark. Her daughter, Mamie Atwood, married Tom Knott, and was the mother of Lewis Atwood Knott, of New York.

Eliza Thruston Rogers married Dr. B. M. Messick, and their only child in Louisville is Martha M. Messick. Anne Thruston Rogers, who married Harvey Yeaman, was the mother of Dr. Rogers Yeaman. Harriet Rogers is Mrs. George Gaulbert, the mother of Carrie Gaulbert, Mrs. Attilla Cox.

Dr. John Thruston married Ellen Pope and was the father of Mrs. Sarah Thruston Hughes, whose children are: Commander William Neal Hughes, U. S. N.; Major Thruston Hughes, U. S. A.; Anabel, Mrs. Garnett Zorn; Katherine Fontaine, Mrs. Walton Maxey, of Beaumont, Texas, and of Dr. Charles Minn Thruston, of Waco, Texas.

Anne Blake Thruston married William J. Johnson, of the pioneer family, and was the mother of Charles Thruston Johnson, who mar-

Thruston

ried first Sally Ward Danforth, and second, Miss Stuart; and of Lizzie Johnson, who married George Breed, and was the mother of Lilla Breed, of Louisville, and George and Edwin Breed, of Boston.

John Thruston, the second son of Charles Minn and Eliza Thruston mentioned above, was a midshipman in the navy at 16, but gave up his commission, returning to Louisville on account of his father's illness. He became a prominent Louisville physician, and during the Civil war was in charge of the Military Hospital at Eighth and Green for nine months.

His brother, Charles Minn Thruston, was a deputy in the county clerk's office, then held by his cousin, Col. Curran Pope. Later he was elected clerk of the county court, filling the position for three terms. He made his residence for a short time in New York, and returned to be re-elected to his former office by a great majority. He was a great political leader and a man of pleasing personality and wide popularity. His wife was Leonora Keller. They had no children.

Capt. Charles Minn Thruston fought in the Revolution, at the age of 11, as aide to his father, the Rev. and Col. Thruston, at the Battle of Piscataway. In 1793 he married Gen. George Rogers Clark's sister, Fanny Clark, after the death of her husband, Dr. James O'Fallon. Their home was at Westport. Capt. Thruston was killed in December, 1800, by Luke, his body servant, who feared that his master would punish him for repeated misdemeanors. Capt. Thruston refused to take Luke on a trip back to Virginia, and warned him that any misconduct during his absence would mean a thrashing. The slave had not attended to his duties during his master's absence, and before the return of Capt. Thruston, ran away. However, one night early in December, a servant reported to Capt. Thruston that Luke had been in the kitchen and had stolen a leg of lamb. Capt. Thruston and his small son went out to look for Luke, tracking him by footprints in the snow. When discovered hiding in a corn shock, Luke sprang on his master and stabbed him with a carving knife which he had stolen from the kitchen. Luke was caught and was hung by verdict of the jury. Capt. Thruston's widow married her cousin, Judge Dennis Fitzhugh, and her home stood in the square between Green and Jefferson, Brook and Floyd.

Capt. and Mrs. Thruston's son was named Charles Minn Thruston, but owing to confusion arising from the name being borne by his cousin, the son of John Thruston, was called Charles W. Thruston. He was a successful manufacturer

Thruston

and merchant, and his wife was Mary Eliza Churchill, daughter of Col. Samuel Churchill. Their daughter, Fanny Thruston, married Andrew J. Ballard, the lawyer. Fanny Thruston Ballard was a great beauty and belle, and died in Vienna in April, 1896, while making a European trip. On this trip she visited the home of the early Thrustons, seeing the old manor house and porter's lodge at West Buckland, England, and an old church nearby, where her ancestors are buried within the chancel.

S. Thruston Ballard and Rogers C. Ballard Thruston are her sons, the name of the latter being changed to preserve the family name of Thruston. S. Thruston Ballard married Sunshine Harris, and has one daughter, Mary Ballard, who married Dr. David Cummins Morton. The late Charles T. Ballard, who married Mina Breaux, was the father of Abigail Ballard, Mrs. Jefferson Stewart; of Charles T. Ballard, U. S. N.; of Fanny Ballard, Mrs. Charles Horner; of Breaux Ballard, whose wife was Jane Fish, and of Mina Ballard, Mrs. Warner L. Jones. The youngest member of the family is little Frances Horner.

"Lansdowne," the home of Mrs. and Mrs. S. Thruston Ballard, at Glenview, bears the name of the early Virginia home of the Thrustons, at Gloucester Point.

Louisville's First Families

Buckner Thruston settled in Lexington in 1788, practiced law and was Judge in the State courts. His wife was Janette January, of Maysville. He was Senator from Kentucky in 1804, and retired to become United States Judge for the District of Columbia. His home from 1804 was at Cumberland, Md.

Gen. Charles Lee, a great personal friend of the Rev. and Col. Charles Minn Thruston, left his library to Buckner Thruston, saying that he was the only man he knew capable of appreciating it.

There are descendants, in Louisville, of the Rev. and Col. Charles Minn Thruston by his second wife, Ann Alexander, their daughter, Eloise Thruston, born 1792, in Virginia, marrying Major Edmund Taylor, and settling on Beargrass. Sarah Courtney Taylor, one daughter, married John De Colmesnil, and their home on Jefferson street, between Eighth and Ninth, was long a landmark of that old neighborhood. Sarah and John Colmesnil's daughter, Courtney Colmesnil, married John Murphy, of Nelson county, for years manager of the Galt House, and has a daughter in Louisville, Mary May Murphy, widow of Joseph Simmons. She is the mother of Courtney Simmons, Lily Simmons Huber, Joseph Simmons and Sarah Thruston Simmons.

Thruston

Sarah Thruston Simmons was instrumental in organizing the Charles Minn Thruston Chapter, Children of the Confederacy in Louisville.

ZACHARY TAYLOR
Twelfth President of the United States and a Major General, U. S. Army, from an old photograph in the possession of Hancock Taylor.

The Taylor Family.

AMONG the most distinguished of the early settlers in Louisville were the Taylor brothers, Col. Richard Taylor, the father of Gen. Zachary Taylor, president of the United States, Hancock Taylor, deputy surveyor under Col. William Preston, and Capt. Zachary Taylor, men of finest Virginia stock, who were prominent actors in the romantic history-making days before Kentucky was a State.

"Hare Forest," four miles from Orange Court House, Va., was the early home of the Taylor family, founded by James Taylor and his wife, Frances, who came from Carlisle, England, in the seventeenth century. James Taylor was a man of affairs, interested in the well being of the colonies, and owning wide acres in Virginia. His only son, James Taylor, who was one of the first surveyor generals, was colonel of Orange county militia, a Knight of the Golden Horse Shoe, and a burgess of King and Queen county, 1702-1714. His wife was Martha Thompson, a daughter of Col. William Thompson, of the British army, whose father, Sir Roger Thompson, served under Cromwell. After Col. Taylor's death, the House of Burgesses ordered Hanover, Spottsylvania, and Orange counties to pay one thousand pounds of tobacco to his widow in recognition of his services in running the boundaries of these counties. James and Martha Thompson were the great grandparents of two presidents of the United States—James Madison and Zachary Taylor. From two sons of James Taylor II., Col. George Taylor and his wife, Rachael Gibson, and Zachary Taylor and his wife, Elizabeth Lee, of the Virginia Lees, are descended a hundred dozen Kentuckians, and from them come the numerous members of the Taylor family in Louisville.

George Taylor was colonel of Orange county militia and fought in Indian wars; Burgess of Orange county, 1748-49, 1752-58; member of Committee of Safety, 1774-75; member of convention in 1775; vestryman of Episcopal church in King George county; Clerk of Orange county for many years. He was the father of ten soldiers of the Revolution, nine of whom were officers. James Taylor was sergeant major of militia, afterward Clerk of Orange county, a position formerly held by his father. Lieut. Jonathan Taylor married Anne Berry, of Gloucester, Va., and settled in Clark county, Ky., in 1789, establishing their home, "Basin Springs." Edmund Taylor was captain, serving on the Virginia State Line; he married Cath-

Taylor

erine Stubbs. Richard Taylor was commodore of the navy and received a thousand acres of land in Kentucky from his country in recognition of his distinguished services. Commodore Taylor lived in Louisville for a number of years before his death in 1825.

Francis Taylor was appointed a captain, but was made colonel of regulars in 1779. Lieut. John Taylor was appointed a midshipman in the navy and died a British prisoner on the old Jersey prison ship. Major William Taylor served through the war, married his cousin, Elizabeth Taylor, came early to Kentucky, and was in Louisville, where he ran a hotel at Second and Main in 1812. He was very popular, and it is said that at his hotel the food was cooked and served in the best old Virginia style. Charles Taylor was sergeant's mate of the Second Virginia army and rose to rank of sergeant of regulars of Convention Guards, Reuben Taylor was a minute man for six years and rose to rank of captain. The tenth son, Benjamin Taylor, served in the navy during the war. Practically all of these men received large grants of lands for military service in the Revolutionary war.

There are no more picturesque figures in the winning of the West than the sons of Zachary Taylor and Elizabeth Lee. Richard Taylor rendered valuable service in the Revolution, and his

WILLIAM BERRY TAYLOR   SUSANNAH GIBSON TAYLOR

These portraits of William Berry Taylor and his wife, Susannah Grayson Harrison Gibson, are owned by their grandchildren, Betty, Fanny and Robert Mallory, of Crescent Hill, whose father, the Hon. Robert Mallory, was a member of Congress and prominent in the social and political life of his day.

William Berry Taylor was a son of Lieut. Jonathan Taylor, Revolutionary soldier, and his wife, Anne Berry. Their home was "Spring Hill" in Oldham county, and from them are descended many members of the Taylor connection in Louisville.

William Berry Taylor was a cousin and a warm personal friend of President Taylor, who frequently visited his kinspeople at "Spring Hill."

Notably among the decendants of William Berry Taylor are Admiral Robert Mallory Berry, U. S. N., a grandson, and Admiral Hugh Rodman, U. S. N., K. C. B., a great-grandson.

Taylor

brother, Hancock Taylor, belonged to Washington's company of Rangers. Both men stood six feet two and weighed about 230 pounds. They made the first trading trip from Pittsburg past the Falls of Ohio to the mouth of the Yazoo in 1769, and the same year from Pittsburg in a canoe made a trip to New Orleans, where they embarked for Charleston, S. C., walking thence to the Taylor home at Orange Courthouse.

Hancock Taylor was one of the early deputy surveyors under William Preston and headed a party, including Willis Lee and Abraham Hapstonstall, known to have made surveys in what is now Jefferson county, in May, 1774. The following year Gov. Dunmore, becoming apprehensive for the safety of the surveyors, ordered their recall, and Hancock Taylor received the summons while laying off a tract near the Kentucky river for Col. William Christian. He was, however, a victim of the Indians and, wounded by a shot from a warrior's rifle, was carried by his companion Hapstonstall to a point near Richmond, where he died and was buried by Hapstonstall, who carved his name on the headstone with tomahawk. Taylor's dying request was that his papers be carried to Preston in Virginia.

Hancock Taylor's will left two-thirds of all his lands lying on Western waters to Hapston-

Louisville's First Families

stall and Willis Lee, and the remainder of his vast estate to his brothers, Col. Richard and Capt. Zachary Taylor.

Col. Richard Taylor, whose wife was Sarah Dabney Strother, came from Orange county, Va., to settle at Falls of the Ohio in the year of 1785, bringing with him his family, including a son, Zachary, aged nine months. Some biographers of this same Zachary, more interested in him, however, as a President of the United States than as a youthful pioneer, claim that Zachary was born at "Montebello," the home of some kinsmen where the Taylors had been detained by illness of some member of their party after leaving "Hare Forest," the ancestral home of the Taylor family.

Col. Richard Taylor established his family in a substantial log house on a farm five miles east of Louisville, which was known as "Springfield." Col. Taylor, who had been through the Revolution as a colonel in the First Regiment of Virginia in the Continental Line, was soon a leader in affairs in both city and State. He was a member of the Convention in Kentucky, 1792-99, and helped frame the first and second constitutions of the State; he was one of the two men selected to have the first courthouse built in Louisville and served on one of the early boards of

Taylor

trustees. He was evidently a man of wealth for he left his family a handsome estate.

Zachary Taylor grew to manhood in the stirring times of frontier clearing with Indian fighting as a matter of every-day life. At eighteen he was a lieutenant in the army and eight years later he served as a major in the War of 1812. The outbreak of the Mexican war found him in command of the American forces in Louisana and Texas, the crowning battle of his campaign being Buena Vista in 1847. Dissatisfied with his treatment by the administration, Major General Taylor resigned and came to Louisville, living on a farm on the Brownsboro road in the months between his retirement from the army and his election as the twelfth President of the United States. He died in office on July 9, 1850.

Zachary Taylor was known to the army as "Old Rough and Ready," because he was ready for any emergency and took the rough end of every encounter, but he was also a man of culture and refinement.

The accompanying sketch of his family places him as a man of gentle birth and breeding, and his connections are with the most distinguished families of Virginia. One who knew him well described him as a man of great tenderness of heart, of gentle manner, devoid of self-assertion;

a silent man, but one whose dignity impressed all who came into his presence. Such was the character of this most distinguished of the Taylor family, whose name has been on every lip since the army cantonment named Camp Zachary Taylor to do him honor was established here.

Zachary Taylor married Margaret Markall Smith, of Maryland, a daughter of Major Walter Smith, U. S. A. To them were born four children: Anne, who married Dr. Robert C. Wood, a surgeon of the United States Army; Sarah Knox married Lieut. Jefferson Davis, afterward President of the Confederacy; Elizabeth married Major William Bliss, U. S. A., and later Philip Dandridge, of Virginia, and the only son was Gen. Richard Taylor, of the Confederate army, who visited England after the war and was given much attention. He moved to New Orleans, married and had three daughters. There are in Louisville no descendants of Zachary Taylor.

Col. Richard Taylor and his wife, Sarah Dabney Strother, had a large family. Their son, Hancock Taylor, married Sophia Hoard and had one son, William Dabney Strother Taylor, who married Jane Pollock Barbour, and whose son, Hancock Taylor, a Confederate veteran, lives in Louisville. His wife was Mary H. Wallace, and their children

Taylor

are: Margaret Barbour, who married Judge Arthur Wallace; Letty Hart, the wife of the Rev. T. P. Grafton, missionary to China; Mary Strother and William P. and Helen Wallace, who married James Quarles, missionary in Argentina.

Hancock Taylor, brother of the President, married again, his second wife being Annah Hornsby Lewis. One daughter was Mary Taylor Robinson, who married Archibald Magill Robinson. Their son, Richard Goldsborough Robinson, married Laura Pickett Thomas, and their children here are Eliza Lee Robinson and Judge Harry Robinson. Another daughter, Mildred Taylor, married John McLean, and their son, Hancock McLean, was the father of Mrs. Louis D. Wallace, of Crescent Hill.

Edmund Taylor, the son of Hancock Taylor, married Lou Barker and was the father of Lewis Taylor, who lives here. Another son was Major Joseph Walter Taylor, who served in the Confederate Army on Gen. Buckner's staff.

He married Lucy Bate and was the father of J. B. Taylor and Jennie Taylor. His second wife was Ellen Bate, and his three daughters, the Misses Taylor, live on the Brownsboro road. Another Confederate soldier in the family of Hancock Taylor was Capt. Samuel Burks Taylor, who was one of the Confederate officers captured and imprisoned with Gen. John Morgan in the Columbus, O., penitentiary. It was Capt. Taylor who scaled the walls and made possible the escape of the prisoners. He was never married.

Elizabeth Taylor, a sister of Gen. Zachary Taylor, married her cousin, John Gibson Taylor, and had several children, only one of whom is known to have a family here. This daughter, Sarah Taylor, who is buried in the old family burying ground at Springfield, was the wife of Col. W. R. Jouett, U. S. A., their children being: Fred Jouett and Lieut. Landon Jouett. Margaret Dudley, who lives here, is a granddaughter. John Gibson Tayor, Jr., was a Confederate soldier who was killed in action in one of the Kentucky battles. Other sisters of Gen. Taylor married prominent men and moved away from Louisville.

"Springfield," the Taylor home of 1785, was a substantial log house to which a brick addition was built, and later a brick house was added to the addition and the log building torn away. Hancock Taylor, the elder brother of Gen. Taylor, had a home on the Eighteenth-street road, but bought out the other heirs' interest in the old place and moved to "Springfield," where he died. Hancock Taylor was in the tobacco business, and as a young man was an Indian fighter.

Taylor

"Springfield" is now owned by Dr. John A. Brady. The monument erected by the government in 1891, in memory of Gen. Taylor, is at "Springfield" burying ground.

Capt. Zachary Taylor, brother of Hancock Taylor and Col. Richard Taylor, married Alice Chew, of the well-known family of that name, and settled on the forks of Hickman creek, in what is now Jessamine county. His daughter, Sarah Taylor, married Richard Woolfolk, a Kentucky pioneer identified with the early history of Jefferson county. It was he who caught Col. William Christian in his arms when that pioneer fell, a victim of the Indians. After the death of his wife Capt. Taylor came to the Woolfolk home, in Jefferson county, eight miles from Louisville, on land between Harrod's creek and the Ohio river.

Samuel Woolfolk, a son of Richard and Sarah Woolfolk, was a well-known lawyer. His wife was Carrie Thornton, by whom he had five sons. Richard Henry Woolfolk, one of these, married Amanda Enders, of Paducah, and their son, Junius Woolfolk, lives in this city.

A son of Lieut. Jonathan and Anne Berry Taylor was William Berry Taylor, born 1768, who married Susannah Grayson Harrison Gibson, settling in Oldham county, then Shelby county, in 1796, on a thousand acres of land bought from his uncle, Col. Francis Berry. They built the home, "Spring Hill," the first brick house in the county, and the home remained in possession of the family until last year. From Spring Hill, Gen. Zachary Taylor, with one of his daughters and with his cousin, Betsy Taylor, who married Dr. William Willett, of the Bullitt family, rode on horseback to Frankfort to attend the first assembly ball, taking their evening clothes in their saddle bags.

Abraham Hapstonstall, the surveyor, spent the declining years of his life in the homes of Hancock Taylor and of William Berry Taylor. He is buried in the Taylor family burying ground at "Spring Hill."

Several of the Revolutionary brothers, sons of Col. George Taylor, were pioneer settlers in Kentucky, and from time to time their descendants have drifted into Louisville from the Bluegrass, from Eastern Kentucky and from the neighboring counties. Among these Kentucky Taylors now in the city are the following:

Mrs. John W. Green, Mrs. Alexander McLennan, Mrs. Jack Langhorne Brent, Judge George Brent, Dr. E. R. Palmer, Mr. Edmund F. Trabue, Miss Alice Trabue, Col. William Colston, Mr. T. P. Taylor, Mrs. E. Polk Johnson, James Berry, Mrs. Robert Brooke, Miss Ruth Rodman, Mrs. Sam Overstreet, Mrs. T. J. Howe, Mr.

Taylor

Horace Hurley, Mr. Frank Barbour, Mrs. James Hegan, Dr. John B. Richardson, Mr. Samuel B. Richardson, Mrs. Harrison Robertson, Mrs. Thos. Kennedy Helm, Miss Addie Meriwether, Mr. Edmund Taylor Meriwether, Mrs. Baylor Hickman, Mrs. Gilbert Garrard, Mrs. Thomas R. Gordon, Mrs. Arthur Peter, Mrs. Karl Jungbluth, Jr., Mrs. J. K. Woodward, Miss Betty Mallory, Miss Fanny Mallory, Mr. Robert Mallory, Dr. R. A. Bate, Mr. Virginius Bate, Mrs. Cora Taylor Russell, Edward G. Isaacs, Mrs. Robert Herr, Mrs. S. E. Frazee, Mrs. Joseph Simmons, Mrs. Herman D. Newcomb, Mrs. Arthur Peter, Darwin Ward Johnson, Mrs. Kate Johnson Lester, Donald Jacob, John I. Jacob, Wallace Taylor Hughes, William B. Eagles, Nannie Lee Frayser, Mrs. Barber Baldwin, Mrs. John Cannon, Dr. and Mrs. John Taylor, Rebecca Taylor, Sallie Taylor, Lucy Catherine Taylor, James Hughes and Mrs. George Grevemeyer. In many instances the members of the Taylor family are descendants of two branches of the family.

"BERRY HILL"

The Bate home at Glenview, built by James Smalley Bate shortly after 1800. The house is a splendid example of farm colonial architecture and is now owned and occupied by Mr. and Mrs. R. Baylor Hickman.

The Bate Family.

"BERRY HILL" was the Virginia home of James Smalley Bate, and for that reason the Kentucky pioneer chose that name for his extensive acreage on the Ohio river, his estate covering the land which is now the suburb of Glenview, and the Bate residence being the Glenview Farms, home of Mr. and Mrs. Baylor Hickman.

Dr. James Bate, a surgeon, who emigrated from Yorkshire, England, and settled in St. Mary's, Maryland, was the father of the Kentucky settler.

Dr. Bate married Susannah Bond, the daughter of James Bond, whose five sons fought in the Delaware Blues. The Bates removed to what is now Martinsburg, W. Va., and it was there that on attaining his majority James Smalley Bate married Lucy Moore Throckmorton, granddaughter of John Robinson, speaker of the House of Burgesses, and great granddaughter of Sir Alexander Spottswood, first Colonial governor of Virginia.

When James Smalley Bate and his family came to Kentucky in 1789, their first location was Harmony Landing on the river above Prospect. They moved shortly to Falls of Ohio, and their first home here was a twelve-room log house on "Berry Hill." The second house was of brick and stood about five hundred yards from the third house on "Berry Hill," which was started shortly after 1800, and is now the Hickman home. The house and grounds were planned and laid out, a composite of the old Bate places in Maryland and Virginia.

James Smalley Bate was interested in the civic life of Louisville, and he was one of the founders of Christ Church Cathedral, and gave the land on which the church was built. He died in 1834, leaving a large fortune to his seven children, each receiving 500 acres of the estate. James Smalley Bate is buried in the old Glenview cemetery and here lies his mother, Susannah Bond Bate, who was born in 1740. Dr. James Bate died in Virginia during the Revolution.

The black walnut forest to the side of the homestead furnished the beautiful wood which is found in the mantels, and the woodwork and floors throughout the dwelling. The forest itself was uprooted in the Louisville cyclone and the side of the house was badly damaged also. According to a tradition in the family, expert carvers were paid $150 apiece for the work on the mantels, which are exquisite in design. The doors

Bate

for the house were brought on packmules from Virginia, and as the house was finished before the doors arrived, it was necessary to hang mattresses in the apertures when the family took possession of the house.

The little attic room in the cupola, high up over the front door, is said to have been the household bank, and here James Smalley Bate kept the treasure chest with its stock of gold from which the expenses of the estate were drawn, and into whose coffers poured the wealth of this substantial and prosperous landholder, who did so much to advance agricultural pursuits in Jefferson county.

Gerard Bond Bate inherited the Bate home, "Berry Hill," and he sold it in 1869 to James C. McFerran, who, with his son, John B. McFerran established a famous trotting horse farm on the Glenview Farms. Later it was the home of John E. Green, and for some years has been owned by the Hickmans.

John Throckmorton Bate, who was born in 1809 at Berry Hill, and lived to be eighty-eight years old, spent his life in that vicinity. In 1834, the year of his marriage, to Eleanor Anne Locke, he built "Woodside" within a mile of his father's home. The house still standing is a splendid example of the Virginia farmhouse colonial of white brick. In this house lived three generations of Bates, the last owner in the family being John Throckmorton Bate, son of Clarence Bate and Octavia Zantziger, and grandson of John Throckmorton Bate.

The name of "Woodside" was changed to "Arden" when the beautiful place was purchased by Peter Lee Atherton, who continues to make it his year-around home. Many fine pieces of mahogany furniture bought for Berry Hill and Woodside are still in possession of the Bate family in Louisville. A quantity of the family silver was lost in a fire a few years ago.

James Smalley Bate and his wife, Lucy Moore Throckmorton, were the parents of the following children: Catherine, James Smalley, Robert, Susan, Lucy, Gerard Bond and John Throckmorton Bate.

Catherine Bate married Henry Washington, a Virginian and close kinsman of George Washington, who as a very young man left the Old Dominion for the Kentucky settlements. No other member of his immediate family ventured this way, and when one of his descendants was seeking an accurate genealogy of the family it was necessary to make a trip to Virginia to secure data from the Washington Bibles.

There are three children of Catherine and Henry Washington living at Irvington, Ky. Mary Washington, who married Theodore Mun-

Bate

ford, recently celebrated her ninetieth birthday; Georgiana, who married Richard Herndon, the mother of Jesse M. Herndon, of Irvington, and Bate Washington, whose wife was Mary Helm. Emmaree Washington, daughter of Bate and Mary Washington, is the wife of B. Perry Weaver, of Louisville, and the mother of Ben Helm Weaver, Burton Perry Weaver and Mary Washington Weaver.

Glorvine Eugenia Washington, daughter of Henry and Catherine, married Alfred Harris, and from her is descended a granddaughter, Catherine Washington Harris, the wife of Dr. Clint W. Kelly. She is the mother of Dr. Alfred Harris Kelly, whose wife was Amy Gunn Snowden before her marriage; Dr. Clint W. Kelly, Jr., Wager Swayne Kelly and Edwin Parson Kelly. Susan Washington, another daughter, married Dr. Joseph Morrison Tydings, the Methodist minister, and their son Richard H. Tydings and his wife, Nell Mansir, with their four children: Joseph Mansir, Anna Ray, Richard, Jr., and Mary Avery Tydings, make Louisville their home.

Lucy Washington married Junius Alexander, and their son, Dr. Junius B. Alexander, lives here.

Lucy Bate, who married George Gray, had five children, but left few descendants. A daughter,

Lizzie Gray, married Mann William Satterwhite, and was the mother of George Satterwhite, who married Laura Hays, and of Bessie Satterwhite, the wife of Walter Stouffer, and mother of Walter Stouffer, Jr.

Mary Gray married Dr. Coleman Rogers, and their only living child is Mary Rogers, Mrs. William O. Andrews, of St. Louis, and the mother of four children. William Gray married Nellie Snowden, and has living here one granddaughter, Eleanor Gray, the wife of Rudolph C. Krauss. Lucy Gray was never married. Ella Gray, one of the four daughters of Lucy Bate and George Gray, is the widow of Norbourne G. Gray, and has one son, Coleman Gray, who makes his home in New York.

Gerard Bond Bate, who inherited the home place, died a bachelor. He was a Harvard graduate, and a man of great culture and refinement.

John Throckmorton Bate married Eleanor Anne Locke, and had two sons, Octavius Bate, who died as the result of an accident while a student at Centre College, and Clarence Bate, who was educated at Brown's, a classmate of Elihu Root and John Hay.

Clarence Bate married Octavia Zantziger, daughter of Major Richard Zantziger, and his wife, Mary Bullitt. There were four children of

Bate

this marriage, three living, Octavius L. Bate, a bachelor; John Throckmorton Bate, who married Margaret Mitchell, and Octavia Zantziger Bate, who is the wife of Dr. Clarence Graves, head of the Baptist Mission of the South, at Nashville.

John Throckmorton and Margaret Bate have two children, Margaret, the wife of Allen Ford Barnes, of San Antonio, and the mother of Margaret Ford Barnes, and John Throckmorton Bate, Jr., a student of medicine at University of Virginia.

Susan L. Bond Bate married in August, 1826, Richard Taylor Robertson, the son of Isaac Robertson, who came from Glasgow, Scotland, and his wife Matilda Taylor, daughter of Commodore Richard Taylor. The Robertsons left Louisville to make Brandenburg their home. They had thirteen children, and from one of these, a daughter, Susan Eliza Robertson, a number of Louisville people are descended. She married her cousin, Richard Alexander Bate, a son of James Smalley Bate II, and his wife, Virginia Alexander.

Susan Eliza and Richard Alexander Bate have a daughter and two sons in the city, Fanny Barbour Bate (Mrs. Theodore S. Drane), Dr. Richard Alexander Bate, who married Julia Hornsby Calloway, a descendant of Daniel

Boone's companion, Col. Calloway, the Indian fighter, and Virginius A. Bate, who married Eliza Johnson.

Lucy Moore Throckmorton Bate, another daughter married Henry Watts Clark, of Chicago, and James Smalley Bate married Nell Semple, a cousin, and lives in Henry county.

James Smalley Bate and his wife, Virginia Alexander, had a family of eight children, and their home was a part of the Glenview Farms. The couple lived there, died there, and their children are making their home on the land. Two daughters, Lucy and Ellen Bate, married Major Walker Taylor, Confederate veteran, and nephew of Gen. Zachary Taylor. From Lucy Bate Taylor, the first wife, are descended James Taylor and his sister, Virginia Taylor, who live on the Bate land on the Brownsboro road. Ellen Bate Taylor, the second wife, leaves three daughters, the Misses Taylor, who also live out on the Brownsboro road. Another daughter of James Smalley and Virginia Bate is Virignia Alexander Bate, who lives on a portion of the old farm.

Robert Bate, son of James Smalley Bate and Lucy Moore Throckmorton, married Fannie Barbour, and had four sons, Gerard Bate, a bachelor; William Bate, who married Lucy Washington; Philip Bate, whose wife was Helen Bullitt, and

Bate

Edward Bate, who married Fannie Mayo, and has two children, Rebekkah Bate Welch, of New York, and Yandell Bate, U. S. A.

COLONEL JOHN FLOYD

Sketched from the photograph of an old picture which hung in Col. R. T. Durrett's library, used to illustrate William Floyd Tuley's "Genealogy of the Tuley and Floyd Families".

Photographs of Colonel Floyd's son and grandson, the John Floyds, who were Governors of Virginia, bear a striking resemblance to this old likeness of the vigorous pioneer.

The Floyd Family. I.

LETTERS written by Col. John Floyd to his chief, Col. William Preston, county lieutenant and surveyor of Fincastle county, Va., present an exceptionally fine picture of how Kentucky was wrested from the Indians and of the early settling of Louisville and of the Central Kentucky towns, but are even more interesting in the light they cast upon their author, John Floyd, pioneer statesman and surveyor, and Kentucky's hero of heroes.

A Virginia gentleman of rare mental attainments, brave as a lion, a true friend, of the warmest affections, Col. Floyd reveals himself in his letters to Col. Preston and to Gen. George Rogers Clark, letters written between 1774 and 1783, the best years and the last years of his life, for at thirty-three Floyd was a victim of the Indians. While comparatively little has been recorded in histories, Floyd's letters are preserved in the Virginia Archives and the Draper MSS., making an authentic memorial to his achievements.

John Floyd was born in 1750, in Amherst county, Va., a son of Col. William Floyd and Abigail (or Abediah) Davis Floyd, and one of a number of children who later emigrated to Kentucky to become founders of Louisville families. Abigail Davis was a sister of Evan Davis, grandfather of Jefferson Davis, according to a tradition in the family, and like her husband was descended from Welsh emigrants to Virginia. In 1772, John Floyd moved to Fincastle county, where he taught school, living in the home of Col. William Preston. Two years later Preston made Floyd a deputy surveyor and appointed him chief of a surveying party to Kentucky, then known as a part of Fincastle county. The party set out on April 7 from Col. Preston's home at 1 o'clock in the afternoon in high spirits, escorted three miles by the surveyor, according to Hanson's Journal, kept by one of Floyd's party, Thomas Hanson, a young gentleman who faithfully set down the traveling experiences of the brave little band. He tells how they received news of battles with the Indians; of meeting up with friends in the forest and having a feast of bear meat; of overtaking Hancock Taylor at the head of another surveying party, and of the men proceeding together in great harmony; of Mr. Floyd laying off two thousand acres of land on Cole river for Col. George Washington; of lands surveyed in Kentucky for Patrick Henry and other prominent men of the time. Floyd's special mission on his first trip was to make survey of the bounty

Floyd

lands offered to veterans of the French and Indian Wars. In that year the activities of the hostile Indians led Dunmore to order the recall of the Virginia surveyors, and Daniel Boone was sent by Preston to order Floyd to bring in his men. On the 26th of August Floyd writes to Preston: "You will hear by Capt. Russell of the death of Mr. Hancock Taylor and one of the company, my poor brother sufferers whose deaths I hope to revenge yet," showing that even this early in his work he had cast his lot with the cause of Kentucky.

Floyd then joined the forces of Gen. Andrew Lewis, but was not in time for the fighting at Point Pleasant. In January, 1775, he was sent back to Kentucky by his chief to make a survey on soldier claims and established the station of St. Asaph. In May he was on Dix river with his party and met up with Lieut. John Henderson, of the Transylvania Company, a settler at Boonesborough, who distrusted Floyd because he represented Col. Preston, whose interests and Henderson's did not coincide. Regarding Floyd, Henderson made the following entry in his journal on May 3, 1775:

"Capt. John Floyd arrived here conducted by one John Drake, from a camp on the Dix river, where he had left about thirty of his company from Virginia. He said he was sent by them to know on what terms they might settle on our lands. This man appeared to have a great share of modesty, an honest, open countenance and no small share of good sense, and, petitioning in behalf of himself and his whole company, among whom were one Mr. Dandridge (Alexander Spottswood Dandridge), and one Mr. Todd, two gents of the law, in their own right, and several other young gents of good family, we thought it advisable to secure them to our interest if possible, and not show the least distrust of the intentions of Capt. Floyd, on whom we intend to keep a strict watch."

However, Floyd effected an understanding with Henderson and did not participate in the land fights that ensued.

In a letter from Boonesborough to Col. Preston, written July 21, 1776, he describes the rescue of the Calloway girls and Daniel Boone's daughter from the Indians, after they had been taken captives from a canoe on the river. He cites this among the Indian depredations, and concludes: "If the war becomes general, which there now is the greatest appearance of, our situation is truly alarming. I want to return as much as any person can do, but if I leave the country now, there is scarcely one single man hereabouts but that will follow my example. When I think of the deplorable conditions a few

Floyd

helpless families are likely to be in, I conclude to sell my life as dear as I can, in their defense, rather than to make an ignominious escape.

"I do, at the request and in behalf of all the distressed women and children, and other inhabitants of this place, implore the aid of every leading man who has it in his power to give them any relief."

But the war was on in earnest and Capt. Floyd returned to Virginia, where he was given charge of the privateer Phoenix, sent out to prey upon British commerce. He sailed to the West Indies and found rich soil, but was captured by the British off the Bahamas and taken to an English prison. After a year as prisoner he escaped, aided by the jailer's wife, made his way to France, where he secured aid of Benjamin Franklin and went home to Virginia.

In 1779 Floyd with his wife, Jane Buchanan, a niece of his friend, Col. Preston, started for Kentucky, making their way to the Falls of Ohio, accompanied or followed by several of his brothers and sisters. He built Floyd's Station, which stood on lands about a mile from St. Matthews. Unfortunately for Floyd and his family, their year at the Falls was one of pitiless cold, always spoken of in history as the "hard winter."

Louisville's First Families

In a letter to Preston, Floyd tells of the weather being "violently hard," of there being no arrivals or news down the river in some weeks. He congratulates Col. and Mrs. Preston on the arrival of their sixth daughter. (Letitia Preston was the bride of John Floyd, Jr., who became Governor of Virginia.) Floyd continues: "I can't buy a bushel of corn for $50, and everything else seems nearly in proportion. Jenny and myself often lament the want of our fine crop of corn the valley of Arcadia, and we both seem to have a fondness yet for that country notwithstanding all the advantages we expect in future. We sometimes laugh at our misfortune with hopes of doing better in a few months, which will soon pass away." In January, Floyd writes again to Col. Preston of the extremity of the settlers at the Falls. "If anybody comes by water I wish we could get a little flour brought down if it was as dear as gold dust. Since I wrote, corn has been sold at the Falls for $165 a bushel. I have sent $600 by Mr. Randolph, a friend of mine, which is for my brother Charles, to purchase some cattle and drive out next spring. We have no prospect of getting any linen. Jenny sends her best wishes and desires to know if it will be possible for Charles to get anything to clothe her and the little boy." Later, May 31: "Do order Charles to bring the net profits of the

Floyd

crop in Arcadia in clothing or we shall be obliged to use fig leaves. The Indians plan to make this neighborhood the seat of war this season. Two men bring accounts that six hundred English with united enemy Indians are now preparing to march against the Falls with artillery. Hardly one week passes without someone being scalped between this and the Falls, and I have almost got too cowardly to travel about the woods without company."

In this year of 1780, Floyd was appointed one of the original trustees of the new city, Louisville, and it is generally supposed that he was also a justice of the peace. His correspondence with Col. Preston during the summer shows the pioneer life as arduous and full of anxiety. In June he writes: "People this year seem generally to have lost their health, but perhaps it is owing to the disagreeable way in which we are obliged to live, crowded in forts, where the air seems to have lost all its purity and sweetness. Our little boy has been exceedingly ill." A postscript to the letter: "Uncle Davis and his son killed near Cumberland Mountains five weeks ago going into settlement. There were four brothers, all of whom have been murdered in seven or eight years. I hear nothing of Charles, and fear if he comes with a small company he will share the fate his uncle and son has done."

Louisville's First Families

In the following year Floyd assumes heavy responsibilities, for in 1781 Gen. Clark wrote Gov. Jefferson, of Virginia, asking him to appoint Col. John Floyd to the position of county lieutenant, describing Floyd as "a gentleman who would do honor to the position and known to be the most capable in the county, a soldier, a gentleman, and a scholar, whom the inhabitants, for his actions, have the greatest confidence in." Floyd was appointed county lieutenant and his letters from this time until his death, to Preston and to Clark, deal with the defense of the fort at the foot of Twelfth street, at Fort Nelson, of militia without ammunition and with horses lost, of the defenseless position of the stations. He writes that the reason that the country is not deserted is due to the fact that the Ohio runs only one way, and that the miserable inhabitants have lost their horses, that the Indians are continually pecking at the settlers, forty-seven inhabitants killed or captured from January to May. In September, Col. Floyd writes Gen. Clark that his company of twenty-seven had been dispersed and cut to pieces, only nine men coming off the field. "A party was defeated yesterday at the same place and many women and children wounded. I want satisfaction; do send me one hundred men, which number with what I can

Floyd

raise, will do. Militia has no good powder, do send some. I can't write—guess at rest."

Col. Floyd appeals to Gen. Clark in May, 1782, in behalf of the inhabitants of Spring Station, who had become so alarmed that they feared to plant their corn without a small guard. They offer their services for work on Ft. Nelson in exchange for a guard of Gen. Clarke's troops for a week's planting. In the same letter he tells of planning to search houses for hemp needed in equipping boats on the river to be employed in fighting the savages, and writes Clark that he and his men have been making rope from "poppaw bark." An earlier letter to Gen. Clark told of preparing canoes ordered by the government, and stated that he, Floyd, was liable for the price of most of them, about four thousand pounds. He writes: "People have been so long amused with promises of paying off indebtedness long incurred that the credit of the State is very little better here than in Illinois." It is understood that Floyd and the other pioneers of means were never remunerated for many of their expenditures of this nature, and practically ruined themselves, giving funds, service, their all, to save Kentucky.

A letter to Col. Preston, in March, 1783, informs him of the death of Billy Buchanan, Mrs. Floyd's brother, at the hands of the Indians. In this letter Floyd observes that he expected something like this to be his own lot. Within a month his apprehension proved true, for on April 10, while riding to the salt works from his station on Beargrass, Col. Floyd was fired upon by Indians and received a mortal wound. In company with him was a brother, whose horse was shot from under him, and a third person, who was killed outright. Col. Floyd was carried by his brother to the salt works, where he died two days later. On April 24 a son was born to Mrs. Floyd, named John, for his father. This John Floyd went back to Virginia to become Governor of the State in 1830, and he was the father of John Buchanan Floyd, elected Governor of Virginia in 1850, and the Secretary of War in 1857 under President Buchanan.

Col. Floyd left two other sons besides his posthumous child, William Preston Floyd, who took up his residence in Virginia, and Capt. George Rogers Clark Floyd, who remained in Louisville to become an Indian fighter like his father.

Floyd county, Floyd's Fork, Floyd street, in this city, are all named for the distinguished gentleman, John Floyd. A drinking fountain on Main street between Third and Fourth was presented to the city, several years ago, by Allen R. Carter through the Sons of the Revolution, as a marker for Floyd's old blockhouse, which stood

Floyd

between Main and the River and Third and Fourth; a monument stands at Eastwood, on the Shelbyville pike, erected a number of years ago to Col. Floyd and his men.

(Copies of Col. John Floyd's letter preserved in the Draper manuscripts and in the Virginia archives are in the library of Mr. Temple Bodley.)

CAPTAIN THOMAS FLOYD SMITH

From a portrait painted when he was a young man and in his uniform of Lieutenant, Eighth Infantry, U. S. A., hanging in the home of his son, Thomas Floyd Smith, at Glenview.

The Floyd Family. II.

WHEN Col. John Floyd came out from Virginia in 1779 to take up his residence near Falls of Ohio, it is said a number of his brothers and sisters journeyed with him or followed him. His correspondence with Col. William Preston, the surveyor of Fincastle county, his lifelong friend and an uncle of his second wife, Jane Buchanan, deals repeatedly with the coming of a brother, Charles Floyd, who was with Col. Floyd at the time of his death.

The parents of the pioneers, Col. William Floyd and his wife, Abediah (or Abigail) Davis, were of Welsh descent, and the family tradition that there is a strain of Indian blood in the Davis family is sustained by old photographs of various descendants, while high cheek bones and blue black hair are noticeable in some generation of each branch of the Floyd connection.

Abediah Davis Floyd, through her father, Robert Davis, who acquired vast properties in Amherst county, Virginia, trading with the Catawba Indians, according to the tradition, was a lineal descendant of Opechancanough, brother of Powhatan, Princess Nicketti, the chieftain's daughter, marrying Nathaniel Davis, of Wales.

Col. William Floyd had one brother, Charles Floyd, who settled in Georgia, the forebear of Major Gen. John Floyd, of Georgia, who was the grandfather of William McAdoo, former Secretary of the Treasury.

Col. John Floyd married in his early manhood a Miss Burwell, of Virginia, who had one daughter, Mourning Floyd, and died shortly after the birth of her child. Mourning Floyd married Col. John Stewart, of Georgia. Ten years after the death of his first wife Col. Floyd married Jane Buchanan, a kinswoman of James Patton, the Louisville settler, according to some accounts.

Three sons were born to John and Jane Floyd, William Preston Floyd, George Rogers Clark Floyd and John Floyd, who was a posthumous child, born twelve days after his father's death. George Rogers Clark Floyd, who was the only one of the three to remain in Louisville, the other brothers going to Virginia, was an Indian fighter. His rank in the army is sometimes given as captain and sometimes as major, but it is known that he commanded a regiment at the battle of Tippecanoe. He was twice married, his first wife being Maria Maupin. Their only son, John Floyd, went to Iowa to locate.

Floyd

Major Floyd's home was near Cherokee Park, where he died in 1821. His declining health was due to the rigors of the campaign against Tecumseh at Fort Harrison.

Major Floyd's second wife, to whom he was married in 1810, was Sarah Fontaine, one of the nine daughters of Capt. Aaron Fontaine.

They had two daughters, Jane and Evelyn Floyd, and the former has a grandson, living in Louisville. Clark Penn, the son of Col. George Floyd Penn, of New Albany, the only known descendant of the illustrious John Floyd, known to make his home here.

John Floyd, who went back to Virginia, married his cousin, Letitia Preston. He studied medicine at the University of Pennsylvania and practiced his profession for a time. Dr. Floyd was elected Governor of Virginia in 1828. His son, John Buchanan Floyd, was Governor of Virginia in 1850, was Secretary of War under Buchanan in 1857, and was a General in the Confederate Army. The first Gov. Floyd had a daughter, Nicketti, who married John W. Johnston, United States Senator from Virginia, and she was the mother of Dr. George Ben Johnston, of Richmond, Va., whose daughters, Nicketti and Helen Johnston, often visit here at the home of Mr. and Mrs. Temple Bodley.

Louisville's First Families

Charles Floyd married Mary Stewart in 1773 in the Hanover Parish church. Their children were pioneer settlers in Indiana. One son was Judge Davis Floyd, prominent in the territorial history of Indiana, while another was Sergt. Charles Floyd, of the Lewis and Clark Expedition, who died on the trip to the coast and was buried at Sioux City, Ia., where a handsome marble shaft marks his grave. This monument was erected by the Floyd Memorial Association, the government contributing $20,000 toward the monument and grounds, known as Floyd Park, commemorating Sergt. Floyd and the Lewis and Clark Expedition.

Isham Floyd, another of the brothers, was killed by the Indians on the Ohio river in 1787.

Nathaniel Floyd, the youngest brother, who married Mollie Thomas in Louisville in 1793, was a soldier in Thomas Joyes' regiment at the battle of New Orleans. After the war Floyd, with several companions, walked through to their homes. He had a farm in the neighborhood of Anchorage, but was living in Louisville at the time of his death in 1840. Two of his daughters have descendants here. Abediah Davis Floyd married Richard Meriwether, and after his death Henry Weaver, of Cincinnati, O. A daughter, Susan Floyd Weaver, married Ernest Gunter, the well-known musician. Mrs. Gunter was

Floyd

much interested in the Floyd genealogy and was a member of the Floyd Memorial Association. She furnished an old letter used in establishing Sergt. Charles Floyd's connection with the Louisville family, a letter written by one of his brothers, Nathaniel Floyd, to his sister, Nancy, telling of Sergt. Floyd's death. This Nancy Floyd married George Rogers and had a daughter, Nancy, who married Judge Wesley Phelps, of Bullitt county. It is believed that the remains of Col. John Floyd repose on the Phelps farm, on the banks of Floyd's Fork, just north of the public road leading from Shepherdsville to Mt. Washington, and about one mile from the former place.

A daughter of Susan Floyd Gunter is Carrie Gunter, who lives in Ivanhoe Court. Ernest Gunter, her brother, makes his home in Kansas City, a civil engineer.

Ann Eliza Floyd, who married George W. Bowling, is the ancestress of Louisville people. Her son, J. W. Bowling, was the father of Pearl Bowling (Mrs. Clay McCandless), and of Blanche Bowling. Mrs. Emma Garvin Harlow, whose mother was Mary Bowling, is the mother of Edna and Nora Harlow and Floyd Preston Harlow.

Elizabeth Floyd, an elder sister of Col. John Floyd, married in Virginia, Charles Tuley, of a

Louisville's First Families

prominent family of Farquier county. The Tuleys decided to make their way to the new settlement and arrived in Louisville in September, 1783. The Tuley family found the other side of the Ohio to their liking, and the family was one of the most prominent and influential in New Albany. The oldest son, William Floyd Tuley, married Jane Bell, daughter of William Bell, of Louisville, having a son, John Wesley Tuley, who married Phoebe Woodruff, daughter of Judge Seth Woodruff, of New Albany. Their son, Enos Seth Tuley, came to Louisville to locate in 1857, and was postmaster of Louisville. He married Mary Eliza Speed, of the pioneer Speed family, and their children in Louisville are Philip Tuley, Dr. Henry Enos Tuley and Thomas Speed Tuley.

Another descendant of the Floyds through the Tuley line is Rose Tuley, who married Charles Earl Currie, of Louisville. Her brothers are Lawrence and Walter Tuley of New Albany.

One sister, Abigail Davis Floyd, married in Fincastle, Va., Thomas Smith, a Virginian, who was killed by the Indians in 1786 at the storming of Brashear's Fort, near Beargrass creek. Their son was Major Thomas Floyd Smith, born in 1784. He was ensign of rifles in 1813 after serving as a second lieutenant in 1812, but he

Floyd

particularly distinguished himself in the Indian wars. He was adjutant to Gen. E. P. Gaines and led the storming party in attack at Ft. Erie. He was breveted major and retired from the army in 1837, living in St. Louis, where he died in 1843.

Major Smith married Emilie Chouteau, a Creole, and one of the daughters of Col. Auguste Chouteau, surveyor of Louisiana, who as a youth of 14, landed at the site of the present city of St. Louis, in charge of the first party of colonists. Col. Chouteau, who superintended the building of the first house in St. Louis, owned an enormous tract of land in the heart of the city at his death, part of which was presented to St. Louis as a park by his grandson, Capt. Thomas Floyd Smith.

Capt. Thomas Floyd Smith, born in 1832 at a Little Rock army post, was appointed a lieutenant in the Eighth Regiment, United States Infantry, in 1855, but resigned in 1858. He was captain of Washington Guards in St. Louis and served under Gen. Frost in the campaign against Kansans in 1861. His home was at Pewee Valley, and his wife was Blanche Weissinger, a descendant of the Bullitts, and his children, who live in Louisville, are Mayor George Weissinger Smith, who married Nell Hunt; Thomas Floyd Smith, president of the

Louisville's First Families

Board of Trade, whose wife was Mary Bruce before their marriage; Amanthus Smith Jungbluth and Nannie Smith, Mrs. Frank Carpenter.

Capt. Smith's brother, Louis Chouteau Smith, of St. Louis, married his cousin, Mary Bullitt, daughter of Alfred and Minerva Beckwith Bullitt. Minerva Beckwith Bullitt was the daughter of John W. Beckwith, of Shepherdsville, and Mary Floyd Smith, the sister of Major Thomas Floyd Smith.

Capt. Smith's sister, Philomena Smith, married Col. Charles P. Larned, U. S. A.

In the possession of Thomas Floyd Smith are a number of papers which belonged to his grandfather, Major Smith. One of these is a letter written October 11, 1839, by Gen. Edward Pendleton Gaines, to Major and Mrs. Smith, "respectfully requesting them to accept a portrait of Edward Pendleton Gaines as a slender token of friendship and in remembrance of unceasing admiration, cherished for twenty-five years, of repeated acts of gallantry by which the then Lieut. Smith, of the First Rifle Regiment, signalized himself and did honor to his corps and his country's service in the defense of Ft. Erie— surpassed by none in the heroic enterprise, displaying the untiring chivalry of a true-hearted patriot."

Floyd

Another letter, beginning "Dear Capt.," was written by Gen. Zachary Taylor at Louisville on January 4, 1824, to Major Smith, dealing with Indian wars, with the political situation and of Major Smith being detailed to command a rendezvous to be established at St. Louis or Belle Fontaine.

The Floyd monument in Shelbyville, which is a fine white marble shaft, bears this inscription. "Erected by the Commonwealth of Kentucky in Memory of Fourteen Brave Soldiers who Fell Under Capt. John Floyd in a Contest With the Indians in 1783."

Although Col. John Floyd was killed April 12, 1783, his will was not probated until 1794, owing to the delay in having survey made of his lands—from the Virginia government. He gave all his lands on the north side of Beargrass to his wife. To his son, Willian Preston Floyd, he gave 2,000 acres on the south side of the creek; to his son, G. R. C. Floyd, a tract of 4,000 acres in Fayette county, and to his unborn son (Gov. John Floyd) he left 1,400 acres on Harrod's creek, ordering the property to be held until the children were of age, and a division of his slaves to be made.

To his brother, Isham, he left 200 acres of Floyd's Fork, and to his brothers, Charles and Robert, 400 acres in any part of his lands they might select on the condition that they complete his surveys and secure patents on all his lands, and with this an equitable division of surveying fees.

www.ingramcontent.com/pod-product-compliance
Lightning Source LLC
Chambersburg PA
CBHW070538170426
43200CB00011B/2465